b r e

delicious home baking recipes

Contents

Text by James Phillips.

This edition published in 2008 by L&K Designs.
© L&K Designs 2008
PRINTED IN CHINA

Publishers Disclaimer

The recipes contained in this book are passed on in good faith but the publisher cannot be held responsible for any adverse results. Please be aware that certain recipes may contain nuts.

Introduction

In today's society, baking has become a popular pastime. Whether it be cakes for a special occasion or just something to fill up the time on a cold winter's afternoon, baking is the "in-thing", along with being easy, cheap and accessible to virtually all households.

But when it comes to baking bread, there are many different varieties which means that whatever the occasion, there is always a fitting recipe. Most bread recipes are based around flour and yeast, meaning that if you stock plenty of these two ingredients, you can easily rustle up hearty, delicious loaves without hours of preparation. And with the invention of bread makers, you can make a loaf of bread at the touch of a button!

Baking is also a great way of getting the family together! Kids will love the thrill of preparing the dough, watching it turn into a tempting loaf of bread and generally getting their hands mucky!

Useful Hints For Baking Bread

Kneading

This is one of the most important parts of bread-making, and ultimately determines how well your loaf will come out. Kneading dough is easy to get the hang of, providing you follow these three easy steps:

1. Make sure your dough has been measured and mixed properly! If there is too much water or flour, it will become very difficult to knead the dough easily. If your dough is still rather sticky, it is advisable to add only 1 or 2 teaspoons of water at a time, to moisten the dough a little but not to ruin it!

2. Lightly flour your hands and your surface. This stops the dough sticking, as the process of kneading is to prevent the dough sticking whilst cooking. Good surfaces to knead on are chopping boards and kitchen worktops (granite worktops tend to work best), but specialy-designed kneading boards are available, which are designed intelligently to stop the bread sticking.

3. Pull the top of the dough over the centre, and then using the heel of your hands, push it away again. Rotate the dough quarterly, and repeat. Once this has been done for approximately 10 minutes, the dough should have become shiny and smooth. A good way to test if your dough is ready for baking is to stretch it into a thin rectangle. If you can do this without any breakages, then it is ready. (N.B Some recipes require longer or shorter kneading times - please refer to specific recipes.)

Following Instructions Carefully
When it comes to baking bread, it is imperative to ensure that all instructions are followed EXACTLY! Even kneading bread for a minute more or less than stated can have a devastating effect on your loaf. Patience is definitely a virtue in breadmaking, and if you get it wrong first time, don't fret! The mistake most often made is rushing through the ingredients and processes, but this can have a serious impact on the quality of your bread.

Testing Your Bread
Knowing when your loaf has risen to the right level and has cooked properly inside can be very difficult to judge, but there are 2 easy ways to test your bread:

1. Looking at it! If your bread appears dry, then it should be done. It should also be pulled away slightly from the sides of the pan and lightly browned on the edges. It is worth slicing it open a little to check inside, however.

2. "The Toothpick Method". Inserting a toothpick into the centre of your loaf is the quickest and most failsafe way to examine your bread. Insert the toothpick approximately 3cm into the loaf, and if it comes out clean, your bread is ready! If, however, batter appears on the toothpick, check regularly using the same method until the pick comes out clean.

It is also important to leave your bread to cool after baking it. Most loaves will require a standing time of around 20 minutes, but again this can vary from recipe to recipe. Leaving your bread to cool enables you to fully savour the taste of the hearty loaf you've just baked! Wire racks are available and are the cheapest and most effective way of allowing your bread to cool after baking,.

What's In It For Me?

Unknown to many people, bread can increase your protein intake, and certain breads contain fibre, part of a healthy diet. And for those weight-conscious out there, bread is a healthy option! It's estimated that there are approximately 75 calories in one slice of white bread, which means that sandwiches, bagels and rolls are great for healthy snacks!

Bread also contains steady levels of Vitamins B1, B2 and B3. Vitamin B1, or Thiamin, is essential for converting blood sugar into energy, and also helps strengthen the nervous, muscular and cardiovascular systems.

Vitamin B2, also known as Riboflavin, is required by the body to aid the metabolism of amino acids and carbohydrates, and can also prevent "weary-eyed fatigue".

Vitamin B3, also known as Niacin, works to counterattack harmful chemicals in the bloodstream, but also aids the creation of hormones in the body, most notably oestrogen in women and testosterone in men.

So, when you're baking bread, not only do you know that you're going to be indulging in a sumptuous loaf full of healthy vitamins and minerals, you'll also be reassured you won't be piling on the pounds!

Bread Machines

Bread machines, also known as bread makers, are appliances used in the home for baking bread. Bread machines became popular roughly 10 years ago in the United Kingdom, and many households now contain one. To the untrained eye, you may wonder how on earth a machine the size of a toaster can make you a loaf of bread! But the simplicity behind it is the reason these wonderful appliances are a must-have in the home!

To create your loaf, ingredients are measured into the pan in a specified order (in most cases, the solids are put in first, followed by liquids) and then the pan is placed in the bread maker. In some cases (for example, making dough for a pizza), you can set the machine to just make the dough, rather than cook your bread. All bread machines come with instructions and it is important to keep hold of these as they will specify which order ingredients should be put into the loaf pan, and which settings need to be used.

International Breads

Pitta Bread (makes 12 pittas)

1½ cups/350ml lukewarm water
¼ cup/175ml shortening (melted)
2 cups/200g all purpose flour/plain
1 cup/150g wholewheat flour
2 tsp instant yeast
1 tsp sugar
1½ tsp salt

1. In a large bowl, combine the lukewarm water and melted shortening. Add in one cup/250ml of flour and the instant yeast. Mix together with a wooden spoon until smooth.

2. Add in sugar, salt and wholewheat flour. Continue to mix together smoothly with a spoon. Continue to add in the rest of the flour.

3. Once the mixture becomes too hard to mix, pour out onto a lightly floured surface and knead for 6 to 7 minutes. The dough should become smooth and elastic. If you are using a stand mixer, knead for 4-5 minutes.

4. Create a ball and leave the dough to rest for 15 minutes. Cover with plastic wrap or a damp cloth. After 15 minutes roll dough into a 12-inch log. Divide the dough into 12 equal portions. Roll each piece into a round ball and cover with a damp cloth for 10 minutes.

5. On a well-floured surface roll out each ball into a 6 inch round disk. Turn dough over only once. Preheat the oven to 450F/230C/Gas Mark 8. If you put a hole in the dough you will not get a pocket in the middle. Place 3-4 pittas on a cookie sheet and bake for 2-3 minutes.

6. Turn over with a spatula and bake for another 2 minutes.

Hawaiian Bread

2 cups/450g granulated sugar
3 cups/300g all purpose flour/plain
1 cup/225g chopped pecans
2 cups/450g mashed ripe banana
1 cup/225g crushed pineapple with juice
1 cup/210ml vegetable oil
½ cup/115ml water
3 eggs
1 tsp salt
1 tsp baking soda
1 tsp cinnamon
2 tsp vanilla extract

1. Preheat the oven to 350F/180C/Gas Mark 4. Place sugar, flour, baking soda and cinnamon into a mixing bowl, stir well. Add the pecans, and mix well again. Reserve at one side

2. In another mixing bowl, beat the eggs. Add the vanilla, salt, pineapple and banana, and mix with a wooden spoon

3. Combine the 2 bowls into one, stirring well until the batter is moistened. Separate the mixture into two floured bread pans.

4. Place in the oven and bake for approximately 1 hour. Leave to cool for 15 minutes.

Bulgarian Buttermilk Bread

1 packet of yeast
5 cups/500g all purpose flour/plain
2 cups/425ml warm buttermilk
1 cup/175g light rye flour
2 tsp oil
2 tsp sugar
1 tsp sour cream
2 tsp caraway seeds
1 tsp salt

1. In a large bowl, dissolve the yeast in the buttermilk. Add the remaining ingredients, mixing the salt with the flours, and work them into dough.

2. Turn the dough out onto a lightly floured surface and knead it for 6 to 7 minutes until the dough is smooth, elastic and glossy. Return dough to greased mixing bowl, turning once to grease top. Cover with plastic wrap and let rise until double in bulk.

3. Preheat the oven to 375F/190C/Gas Mark 5. Divide the dough into 2 equal halves and shape each piece into a round loaf. Set the loaves on a baking sheet that has been slightly dusted with cornmeal.

4. Cover the loaves with plastic wrap and let them rise again for 50 minutes. Bake in the oven for 45 minutes, or until golden brown.

5. Remove the loaves from the baking sheet at once and allow them to cool on a wire rack.

International

Naan Bread

3 cups/300g all purpose flour/plain
¼ cup/40g sesame seeds
½ tsp baking powder
½ cup/115ml yoghurt
½ cup/115ml milk
1 egg
1 tbsp oil
2 tbsp butter
¼ tsp sugar
Salt to taste

1. Sieve the flour and baking powder. Add salt, sugar, yoghurt, oil and butter and mix well for 2-3 minutes. Add the egg and mix for an extra 2 minutes.

2. Add milk and water (if required) a little at a time and knead the dough until it turns very smooth. Cover it with a damp cloth and set aside for at least 2 hours.

3. Preheat the oven to 350F/180C/Gas Mark 4. Divide the dough into medium size balls of equal portions. Roll the ball with a few sesame seeds, apply some flour and roll into thick circular shape.

4. Place on a greased baking tray and cook until golden brown on both sides (check every 5 minutes).

Cut it into two parts diagonally for effect.

Mexican Cornbread

3 cups/500g cornmeal
½ cup/55g all purpose flour/plain
2 tsp baking soda
2 tsp salt
2 tbsp sugar
3 eggs, beaten
2½ cups/275ml of buttermilk
½ cup/110ml olive oil
1 large onion
½ tsp garlic powder
2 jalapeno peppers, finely chopped
2 tbsp chopped pimiento
2 rashers crispy bacon
1½ cups/275g grated Parmesan

1. Have all ingredients at room temperature. Chop the onion and the jalapenos finely. Crumble the bacon. Mix together the cornmeal, flour, soda, salt, and sugar in a large bowl, mixing well.

2. In a separate bowl, whisk together the buttermilk, beaten eggs, and oil. Add to the dry ingredients and mix well for a minute. Don't beat the dough - just stir enough to moisten completely.

3. Fold in the onion, garlic powder, jalapenos, pimiento, bacon, and cheese quickly. Bake in a cast iron skillet at 400F/210C for 25 to 30 minutes, until the top is browned.

Portugese Sweet Bread (Pao Doce)

2 packets of active dry yeast
¼ cup/55ml of warm water (approx. 125F/50C)
1 cup/230ml lukewarm milk (scalded, then cooled)
¾ cup/150g of brown sugar
1 tsp of salt
3 eggs
½ cup/110g softened butter
5½ cups/550g all purpose flour/plain
1 egg

Portugese Sweet Bread/Cont.

1. Dissolve yeast in warm water in large mixing bowl. Stir in milk, ¾ cup sugar, salt, 3 eggs, margarine and 3 cups flour. Beat until smooth.

2. Stir in enough remaining flour to make dough easy to handle. Turn dough onto lightly floured surface. Knead until smooth and elastic, about 6 minutes.

3. Place in a lightly greased bowl. Turn greased side up. Wrap and let rise in warm place until doubled in size, should take approximately 2 hours. (Dough is ready if an indentation remains when touched)

4. Punch down dough and divide into halves. Form each half into a round, slightly flat loaf. Place each loaf in greased round 9x2 inch layer cake pan. Cover and let rise until doubled in size, about 1 hour.

5. Heat oven to 350F/180C/Gas Mark 4. Beat 1 egg slightly and brush over loaves. Sprinkle with 1 tsp sugar. Bake for 35-40 minutes, until loaves are golden brown.

Italian Easter Bread

Bread:
1 packet dry yeast
¾ cup/170g butter, softened
¾ cup/200g granulated sugar
1/3 cup/75ml milk
½ tsp salt
1 tbsp grated orange rind
1 tbsp crushed aniseed
4 eggs
1 egg yolk
¼ cup/65ml warm water (105F/40C)
5 cups/500g all purpose flour/plain
1 cup/150g raisins

Topping:
½ cup/125g granulated sugar
¼ cup/25g all purpose flour/plain
¼ cup/55g butter, softened
2 tbsp almond paste
1 egg white, beaten
¾ cup/60g ground almonds
Confectioners sugar

1. Blend the yeast with warm water and allow 5 minutes for it to dissolve. Add butter, sugar, milk, salt, orange rind, aniseed, eggs and egg yolk. Add 2 cups of the flour and beat for 10 minutes.

2. Add 1 cup flour and beat at low speed. Add 2 cups flour, stirring until well blended. Cover bowl tightly with plastic wrap and allow to rise for 2 hours.

3. Punch dough down, turn out onto floured surface and knead for 10 minutes. Gently knead in raisins.

4. Divide dough into 2 balls. Form two 9 inch flattened rounds on a greased baking sheet. Cover lightly with greased plastic wrap and allow to rise until "puffy" (40 to 45 minutes).

Topping:

5. Blend sugar, flour, butter and almond paste and beat with electric mixer until mixture resembles coarse crumbs. Brush top of rounds with egg white and water mixture. Place topping over loaves; then sprinkle with almonds.

6. Bake in preheated 350F/180C/Gas Mark 4 oven for about 30 minutes. Serve warm, dusted with confectioners sugar.

New England Apple Cheddar Bread
2/3 cup/125g granulated sugar
2 cups/220g self-rising flour
1 tsp ground cinnamon
½ cup/55g chopped cashews
2 eggs, slightly beaten
½ cup/115g butter, melted
1 small baking apple, peeled and finely chopped
Sprinkle of cheddar cheese, grated
¼ cup/65ml milk

1. Preheat oven to 350F/180C/Gas Mark 4. Butter a 9 x 5-inch loaf pan. In a large bowl combine the sugar, flour, cinnamon and cashews.

2. In a separate bowl combine eggs, butter, apples, cheese and milk. Add to sugar mixture.

3. Spread batter into the prepared pan. Bake for 1 hour.

Irish Oatmeal Soda Bread

$\frac{3}{4}$ cup/100g wholemeal flour
$\frac{1}{4}$ cup/30g all purpose flour/plain
$\frac{1}{4}$ cup/30g pinhead oatmeal
2 tbsp wheatgerm
1 tsp bicarbonate of soda
1 tsp salt
1 tsp sugar
1 large egg
1 cup/230ml buttermilk
A little extra flour for dusting

1. Preheat the oven to 375F/190C/Gas Mark 5. Begin by placing the dry ingredients in a large bowl, mix to combine, then beat the egg and buttermilk together and add them to the dry ingredients.

2. Start mixing, first with a spoon, then finish off with your hands to form a smooth dough. Transfer the dough to the loaf tin and level the top.

3. Sprinkle the dough with flour and bake in the centre of the oven for 50-60 minutes.

4. Turn onto a wire rack and allow to cool for 15 minutes.

Jamaican Jungle Bread

1½ cups/150g all purpose flour/plain
1 packet quick oats
½ cup/110g granulated sugar
1 tsp baking powder
1 tsp baking soda
1 tsp cinnamon
½ tsp salt
½ cup/110g flaked coconut
½ cup/75g toasted nuts
3 bananas
1 can of pineapple chunks
¼ cup/55ml vegetable oil
2 eggs

1. Preheat oven to 350F/180C/Gas Mark 4. Grease a 9 x 5 x 3-inch loaf pan. In a large bowl, stir together first 9 ingredients, adding them in order.

2. In a medium bowl, mix bananas, pineapple, oil and eggs; add all at once to oat mixture. Stir just until liquid is absorbed and mixture is thoroughly moistened (do not over mix).

3. Pour the combined mixture into prepared loaf pan and bake for 50 minutes. Allow to cool in pan for 5 minutes, then remove from pan and cool completely.

Spanish Passover Bread

½ peeled potato, diced
1 cup/220ml boiling water
2 eggs
3 tbsp butter at room temperature
1 tsp shredded lemon peel
¾ cup/180g sugar
1 tsp salt
4 cups/900g bread flour
3 tsp instant yeast
1 cup/225g raisins
1 beaten egg for glaze

Spanish Passover Bread/Cont.

1. In a small saucepan over low heat, cook diced potato in the boiling water approximately 10 to 15 minutes or until tender when pierced with a fork. Remove from heat and drain, reserving potato liquid.

2. Add enough water to potato liquid, if necessary, to equal 3/4 cup of liquid. Mash potato with fork. Place mashed potato, 3/4-cup potato liquid, eggs, butter, lemon peel, sugar, salt, bread flour and yeast in a large bowl.

3. When dough is fluffy and light, remove dough from bowl and turn out onto a lightly oiled surface. Form dough into an oval, knead for 4-5 minutes, and cover with a plastic wrap and let rest for 10 minutes.

4. Shape dough either into a large baguette loaf or two small round loaves and place on large baking sheet dusted with flour. Cover with plastic wrap and place in a warm spot to rise, approximately 20 minutes.

5. Preheat oven to 350F/180C/Gas Mark 4. After rising, slash the bread with a bread razor or a very sharp knife making three 1/2-inch deep diagonal slashes on loaf shape or a cross on rounds.

6. Brush top of loaves with beaten egg and bake for 30 to 35 minutes. After 15 minutes, cover loaves with aluminium foil to prevent over browning.

7. Remove from oven and place the bread on a wire rack to cool. Let baked loaf cool for 30 minutes before cutting (this is because the bread is still cooking while it is cooling).

Serve with a selection of fruit.

Bagels

2 tsp active dry yeast
1 cup/230ml warm milk (110F)
4 tbsp softened margarine
2 tbsp sugar
1 tsp salt (enough to sprinkle lightly)
1 egg yolk
2 cups/200g all purpose flour/plain

1. In a mixing bowl, dissolve yeast in warm milk. Put in the butter, salt, sugar and egg yolk, and mix well. Stir in enough flour to form soft dough. Turn onto a floured surface; knead until smooth and elastic for about 8 minutes.

2. Place in a greased bowl, turning once to grease top. Cover with Clingfilm and let rise in a warm place until doubled in size. Punch dough down and shape into 12 balls. Push thumb through centres to form a 1-inch hole.

3. Place on a floured surface. Cover and let rest for 10 minutes and then flatten. In a large saucepan, bring water to a boil. Drop bagels, one at a time, into the boiling water.

4. When bagels float to the surface, remove with a slotted spoon and place 2 inches apart on greased baking sheets. Bake at 450F/230C/Gas Mark 8 for 20 minutes or until golden brown.

Remove from pans, place on wire racks and allow bagels to cool.

St. Joseph's Bread (Pane di San Giuseppe)
2 cups/200g all purpose flour/plain
½ tbsp active dry yeast
1 tbsp honey
2/3-cup hot water
½ tsp salt
2 tbsp butter
3 tbsp aniseed
1/3 cup golden raisins
Cornmeal

1. Combine 1 1/2 cups of the flour, yeast, honey, water, salt, butter and aniseed in a large bowl and mix thoroughly. Add raisins and beat for another 10 minutes, adding flour until the dough begins to pull away from the sides of the bowl.

2. Turn out on a lightly floured surface. Knead for 8 to 10 minutes, until dough is smooth and elastic, adding flour as necessary to prevent stickiness.

3. Lightly oil a large bowl. Place dough in bowl and turn to coat on all sides. Cover with plastic wrap and place in a warm, draft-free place until doubled in size, which should take about 1 hour.

4. Grease a baking sheet and sprinkle with cornmeal or line one with greaseproof paper. Punch down the dough and shape into a long loaf.

5. Place the loaf on the baking sheet and make three or four 1/2-inch diagonal slashes on the top. Cover with a tea towel and let rise until doubled in size.

6. Heat the oven to 350F/180C/Gas Mark 4. Mist loaves with water or vinegar before baking and twice during baking. Bake for about 40 minutes.

Transfer to a wire rack to cool.

Fruit-based Breads

Mango Bread

2 cups/200g all purpose flour/plain, sifted
2 tsp cinnamon
2 tsp baking powder
½ tsp salt
1 cup/230g granulated sugar
2 eggs
¾ cup/135ml of oil
2½ cups/300g of chopped mango
1 tsp lemon juice
½ cup/100g of raisins

1. In a small bowl, combine first 5 ingredients and mix for a minute or so. In a separate bowl, beat the eggs, then add oil, and add this mixture to the first bowl.

2. Preheat the oven to 350F/180C/Gas Mark 4. Add mango, lemon juice and raisins to the mixture and mix thoroughly.

3. Turn into 2 greased loaf pans and bake for approximately one hour, or alternatively, place a wooden pick into the centre, and when this comes out clean, the bread is ready.

Fruit

Banana Bread

1/3 cup/75g brown sugar
1/3 cup/75g granulated sugar
1/3 cup/75g Sunsweet Lighter Bake
2 large eggs
2 bananas, mashed
2 cups/200g all purpose flour/plain
1 tsp baking powder
1/3 tsp baking soda
1 cup/220g chopped walnuts (optional)

1. Preheat the oven to 350F/180C/Gas Mark 4. Coat 9x5-inch loaf pan with cooking spray and set aside.

2. Beat together the sugars, Sunsweet Lighter Bake, eggs and banana. Combine the flour, baking powder, baking soda and stir into batter until just moistened.

3. Stir in the walnuts (if desired). Spoon the batter into the pre-prepared pan. Bake in oven for 55 to 60 minutes. Allow to cool for 10 minutes. Remove from pan and cool completely on rack.

Pineapple Spice Loaf

2 cups/200g all purpose flour/plain
2 tsp baking powder
1 tsp salt
½ tsp baking soda
½ tsp ground ginger
½ tsp ground nutmeg
1/3 cup/80g brown sugar
½ cup/110ml vegetable oil
2 eggs
1 cup/225g crushed pineapple in juice

1. In a large bowl, sift together first 6 ingredients, then stir in brown sugar.

2. In a small bowl, mix oil and eggs until well blended. Stir in pineapple. Bake at 350F/180C/Gas Mark 4 for 55 to 60 minutes.

Pear Bread

3 cups/300g all purpose flour/plain
1 tsp baking soda
1/3 tsp baking powder
1 tsp salt
1 tbsp ground cinnamon
1 cup/220g chopped pecans
2/3 cup/150g vegetable oil
3 eggs, slightly beaten
2 cups/450g granulated sugar
4 peeled and grated pears
2 tsp vanilla extract

1. Preheat oven to 325F/160C/Gas Mark 3. Combine first six ingredients in a large bowl and mix thoroughly. Make a well in center of mixture.

2. Combine remaining ingredients and add to dry mixture, stirring just until moistened. Spoon into two greased 8 x 4-inch loaf pans.

3. Bake for approximately 65 minutes or until done. Cool for 10 minutes before removing from pan.

4. Remove loaf from pan and leave on a wire rack to cool completely.

Praline Apple Bread

1 cup/230g granulated sugar

1 carton dairy sour cream

2 eggs

2 tsp vanilla extract

2 cups/200g all purpose flour/plain

2 tsp baking powder

½ tsp baking soda

½ tsp salt

2 chopped and peeled tart apples

1 cup/220g chopped pecans

½ cup/120g butter or margarine

½ cup/100g packed brown sugar

1. Preheat the oven to 350F/180C/Gas Mark 4. Grease a 9 x 5-inch loaf pan. In a large mixing bowl beat together granulated sugar, sour cream, eggs and vanilla extract on low speed of an electric mixer until combined, then beat on medium speed for 2 minutes.

2. Stir together the flour, baking powder, soda, and salt, then add to sour cream mixture, beating on low speed until combined.

3. Stir in apple and 1/2 cup of the pecans. Turn into prepared loaf pan. Sprinkle with remaining chopped pecans and press lightly into batter.

4. Bake for 55 to 60 minutes (If necessary, cover loosely with foil the last 10 minutes of baking to prevent over-browning.) Cool in pan on a wire rack for 10 minutes.

Rum Glazed Fruit Bread

Bread:

2½ cups granulated sugar

2½ cups mashed bananas

3 eggs

1 small can crushed pineapple

3/4 cup vegetable oil

2½ cups/250g all purpose flour/plain

½ tsp salt

1 tsp baking soda

1 cup/125g chopped pecans

1 tsp vanilla extract

Handful of drained and chopped maraschino cherries

Rum Glaze:

½ cup/125g butter

1 cup/220g granulated sugar

½ cup/125ml rum

1/4 cup/65ml water

Bread:

1. Preheat oven to 300F/150C/Gas Mark 2. Grease a tube pan and dust lightly with flour.

2. Mix sugar, bananas, eggs, pineapple, oil and cherries. Mix well for 2-3 minutes. Combine flour, salt and soda and stir into first mixture. Add nuts and vanilla extract, then mix well.

3. Pour dough evenly into the pan. Bake for one hour and 45 minutes. Cool on a wire rack.

Glaze:

4. In a saucepan, combine ingredients, bring to a boil and boil for 3-4 minutes.

5. Pour half of the glaze over the bread while still in the pan. Allow to cool, then turn cake onto plate and pour remaining glaze over the top.

Fruit

Strawberries 'n' Cream Bread

$\frac{1}{2}$ cup/120g butter, softened

3/4 cup granulated sugar

2 eggs

$\frac{1}{2}$ cup/120g sour cream

1 tsp vanilla extract

2 cups/200g all purpose flour/plain

$\frac{1}{2}$ tsp baking powder

$\frac{1}{2}$ tsp baking soda

$\frac{1}{2}$ tsp salt

$\frac{1}{2}$ tsp ground cinnamon

3/4 cup/175g chopped fresh strawberries

3/4 cup/175g chopped walnuts, toasted

1. In a mixing bowl, cream butter and sugar until fluffy. Beat in eggs, one at a time, mixing throughout. Add the sour cream and vanilla extract, and mix well.

2. Combine the flour, baking powder, baking soda, salt and cinnamon, and stir into creamed mixture just until moistened. Fold in strawberries and walnuts, and pour mixture into a greased 8 x 4-inch loaf pan.

3. Sprinkle with remaining nuts, before baking at 350F/180C/Gas Mark 4 for 65 to 70 minutes. Cool for 10 minutes and remove from pan to a wire rack to cool completely.

Sugar Plum Bread

1 1/3 cups/275g granulated sugar
2 2/3 cups/270g all purpose flour/plain
1 tbsp baking powder
2 tsp pumpkin pie spice
1 cup/225g chopped pecans
4 plums, chopped
1 tsp salt
3 eggs
1 cup/220ml vegetable oil

1. Combine sugar, flour, baking powder, pumpkin pie spice and salt in large bowl. Mix thoroughly and set aside.

2. Combine eggs, oil and plums in a separate bowl. Stir liquid mixture into dry ingredients, mixing until moistened, before folding in the pecans.

3. Divide batter evenly between two 8 x 4-inch ungreased loaf pans. Bake in preheated 350F/180C/Gas Mark 4 oven for 45 to 55 minutes.

Blueberry Orange Bread

2 cups/200g all purpose flour/plain
1 tsp baking powder
½ tsp salt
½ tsp baking soda
½ tsp grated orange peel
2 tbsp butter
1/4 cup/60ml boiling water
1 egg, slightly beaten
1 cup granulated sugar
½ cup/125ml orange juice
1 cup/230g fresh blueberries

1. Heat oven to 350F/180C/Gas Mark 4. Grease the bottom and 1 inch up the sides of an 8 x 4-inch loaf pan, and set aside.

2. In a large bowl, stir together flour, baking powder, salt, baking soda and orange peel, before making a well in centre and set aside.

Blueberry Orange Bread/Cont.

3. Stir together butter and boiling water until butter is melted. In a medium bowl, combine egg, sugar and orange juice, and stir into the butter mixture. Add to the dry ingredients, stirring just until moistened.

4. Fold in the blueberries. Spoon the batter into the prepared pan, and bake for about 60 minutes. Allow to cool for 10 minutes before removing loaf from pan. Cool completely on a wire rack. Wrap in foil and store overnight.

Taffy Apple Bread

1 bag of caramels
3 peeled Granny Smith apples, cored and chopped
3 cups/300g all purpose flour/plain
6 eggs
1 cup/230g butter, softened
4 cups/900g confectioners sugar
1 tbsp vanilla extract
2 tsp ground cinnamon
2 tsp ground allspice

1. Heat oven to 350F/180C/Gas Mark 4. Grease and flour two 9x5-inch loaf pans and set aside.Unwrap the caramels and, using scissors, cut each into eight pieces. Toss with 1 tablespoon of the flour in a small bowl to prevent them from sticking together; set aside.

2. Using an electric mixer, beat the butter, sugar and vanilla extract until fluffy. Add the eggs, one at a time, beating well after each. In another bowl, stir together the remaining flour, cinnamon and allspice.

3. Add the flour mixture to the butter mixture and blend well. Using a wooden spoon, stir in the apples and caramel pieces. Divide evenly between the prepared loaf pans.

4. Bake for 1 hour and 15 minutes or until a wooden pick inserted into the centre comes out clean. Cool completely on a wire rack and then remove from pans.

Lime Bread

3 cups/300g all purpose flour/plain
3/4 cup/180g granulated sugar
3 tsp baking powder
1 tsp salt
1/4 tsp baking soda
1½ cups/300ml milk
1 beaten egg
1/4 cup/65ml vegetable oil
1/4 cup/75ml lime juice
2 tsp grated lime peel
2 tbsp granulated sugar
1 tbsp lime juice

1. Preheat the oven to 350F/180C/Gas Mark 4. Grease a 9 x 5 x 3-inch loaf pan and set aside.

2. In a mixing bowl, stir together flour, sugar, baking powder, salt and baking soda. In a separate bowl, combine milk, egg, oil, the lime peel and lime juice. Add to dry ingredients once mixed well. Stir just until moistened.

3. Turn into prepared loaf pan and bake for 1 hour. Allow to cool in pan for 10 minutes. Remove from pan onto rack.

4. Combine the 2 tablespoons sugar and the 1-tablespoon lime juice. Spoon over top of loaf. Allow to cool completely. Wrap well and store overnight.

Fruit

Orange Bread

3 cups/300g all purpose flour/plain
½ cup/120g granulated sugar
2 tsp baking powder
1 tsp salt
1 cup/225ml milk
1 egg
1 tbsp butter
Rind of 1 orange, boiled and cut into very small pieces

1. Preheat the oven to 325F/160C/Gas Mark 3. Beat the egg, and then add milk. Sift the flour, sugar, baking powder and salt together and add to egg-milk mixture.

2. Add melted butter and orange rind to make a stiff dough. Knead the dough on a lightly floured surface for 3 minutes. Put the mixture into loaf pan and allow to rise for 20 minutes.

3. Bake for approximately 50 minutes, but it is worth checking every 5 minutes after. Allow to cool for 10 minutes before removing, then place on a wire rack to cool completely.

Sour Cream Banana Bread

2/3 cup/180g butter
1½ cups granulated sugar
2 eggs
3 bananas, sliced
2¼ cups flour
1 teaspoon baking powder
1 teaspoon baking soda
½ teaspoon salt
½ cup/115ml sour cream
1 cup/225g chopped walnuts (optional)

1. Preheat the oven to 375F/190C/Gas Mark 5. Sift the cream, butter and sugar until light and fluffy. Add eggs and bananas and beat until well blended.

2. Sift together flour, baking powder, soda and salt. Add to the banana mixture, stirring just to blend. Add the walnuts, stirring them in well.

3. Spoon batter into greased and floured loaf pan. Bake in oven for 90 minutes

Peaches and Cream Bread

Bread:
12 white rolls, thawed and risen
1 cup/225g cream cheese
2 tbsp granulated sugar
2 tsp flour
1 egg yolk
½ tsp vanilla extract
1 can sliced peaches, drained and thinly sliced

Topping:
1 cup/160ml sour cream
3½ tbsp granulated sugar
1 tsp vanilla extract
Fresh peach slices, if desired

1. Press 6 rolls together and roll into a 10-inch circle. Place in a 9-inch spring form pan sprayed with non-stick cooking spray.

2. Beat together cream cheese, sugar, flour, egg yolk and vanilla extract. Spread evenly over dough. Arrange peaches evenly over cream cheese mixture.

3. Press remaining 6 rolls together and roll into a 10-inch circle. Place over peaches. Cover with sprayed plastic wrap. Let rise until double. Remove wrap and bake at 350F/180C/Gas Mark 4 for 15 minutes.

4. With a sharp knife, make several slits in top layer. Bake for an additional 15 to 20 minutes.

Fruit

Papaya Bread

1 cup/225g granulated sugar
½ cup/110g butter
2 eggs
2 ripe papayas
½ cup/110g chopped walnuts
½ cup/110g raisins
1½ cups/150g flour
1/4 tsp baking powder
1 tsp baking soda
½ tsp salt
½ tsp ground cinnamon
½ tsp ground allspice
½ tsp ground ginger

1. Cream together the sugar and butter until light. Add eggs and beat until fluffy. Add the papaya, nuts and raisins and mix thoroughly.

2. Sift together flour, baking powder, baking soda, salt, cinnamon, allspice and ginger and then add to butter mixture.

3. Pour batter into a 9 x 5-inch loaf pan coated in a non-stick cooking spray. Bake at 325F/160C/Gas Mark 3 for about 65 minutes.

Sweet Breads

Sweet

Shortbread Sheep

2 cups/450g unsalted softened butter
1 cup/190g granulated sugar
4 cups/450g self raising flour
¼ tsp salt

1. Cream butter and sugar in large mixer bowl until light and bouncy. Beat in flour and salt. Knead the dough briefly until smooth and flat. If dough is too sticky, add a tiny bit more flour.

2. Heat oven to 350F/180C/Gas Mark 4. Have ungreased baking sheets ready. Pat half of the dough out on lightly floured surface to 1/2-inch thickness. Use cookie cutters to cut out desired shapes.

3. Place cookies 2 inches apart on baking sheets. Bake until light brown on edges, which should take between 20 to 25 minutes. Cool on wire racks.

Note: A sheep pattern can be made out of cardboard and placed over dough, cut out the shape with a small knife.

Honey Wheat Bread

2 tsp rapid rise yeast
½ cup/120ml warm water (approximately 110F/45C)
1 tsp white sugar
1 can of evaporated milk
1/4 cup/60ml water
50g melted shortening
2 tsp/10g salt
1 cup/135g whole-wheat flour
2 cups/190g bread flour
4 tbsp butter

1. Dissolve yeast and sugar in ½ a cup of warm water. Combine milk, ¼ cup water, shortening, honey, salt and wheat flour in food processor or bowl. Mix in yeast mixture, and leave to rest for 10-15 minutes. Add the white flour and mix until the dough forms a ball. Knead dough for about 10 minutes. Place the dough in a buttered bowl, and roll dough around the bowl to cover in butter.

Honey Wheat Bread/Cont.

2. Cover the bowl with clingfilm. Let dough rise for 40-50 minutes, or until size has almost doubled.

3. Divide dough into 2 halves. Roll out each half and puncture all the bubbles. Form into loaves, and place in bread pans.

4. Butter the tops of each dough loaf, and cover loosely with clingfilm. Let it rise until size has doubled again, this second rise should only take 25-30 minutes.

5. Place a small pan of water on the bottom shelf of the oven, and preheat oven to 375F/190C/Gas Mark 5. Bake for approximately 30 minutes, or until tops are dark golden brown. Butter crusts while bread is warm, slice when cool.

Double Chocolate Bread

$2\frac{1}{2}$ tsp dry yeast
$\frac{1}{2}$ tsp sugar
$\frac{1}{4}$ cup/55ml warm water
$4\frac{1}{2}$ cups/450g all purpose flour/plain
$\frac{1}{2}$ cup/110g plus 2 extra tbsp sugar
$\frac{1}{4}$ cup/55ml unsweetened cocoa powder
2 tsp salt
$1\frac{1}{4}$ cups/300ml warm water
12 chocolate squares
Egg wash (one egg plus 1 tablespoon water mixed together)

1. Stir yeast and $\frac{1}{2}$ teaspoon sugar into $\frac{1}{4}$ cup warm water and pour into a large mixing bowl, and let stand until bouncy and foamy, takes about 10 minutes.

2. Mix flour, remaining sugar, cocoa and salt. Stir remaining cups of water into dissolved yeast, then stir in the flour mixture. Stir in chopped chocolate last.

3. Knead on lightly floured surface until smooth and elastic, usually takes 8 to 10 minutes.

4. Place dough in greased bowl, cover with clingfilm and let rise until doubled in size, may take 1 hour.

5. Turn risen dough onto lightly floured surface, punch it down (the chocolate will be very gooey - resist licking your hands until you're done!) and divide in half.

6. Form each half into desired shape and place on greased baking tray. Cover with plastic wrap again and let dough rise until doubled in volume. Meanwhile, preheat oven to 450F/230C/Gas Mark 8.

7. Brush loaves with egg wash and bake in the oven for 10 minutes, then reduce the heat to 350F/180C/Gas Mark 4 and bake for 30 minutes more or until bread sounds hollow when bottom is tapped.

Allow cooling for 10 minutes, you can serve with sweetened cream cheese if desired.

Lemonade Bread

½ cup/110g shortening
½ cup/220ml lemonade
1 cup/225g granulated sugar
2 eggs
¼ cup/55ml milk
¼ cup/55ml lemonade concentrate
1½ cups/150g all purpose flour/plain
2 tsp baking powder

1. Cream together the shortening, sugar and eggs in a large bowl. Add milk and the 1/4 cup lemonade concentrate.

2. Sift together flour and baking powder. Add to the previous mixture. Bake at 350F/180C/Gas Mark 4 for 60 minutes in loaf pan. Allow to cool for 10-15 minutes.

Pina Colada Bread

4 eggs
1¼ cups/290ml olive oil
2 cups/380g granulated sugar
1 tsp coconut extract
1 tsp vanilla extract
1 tsp orange extract
¼ cup/60ml pineapple juice, drained from crushed pineapple
½ tsp grated orange zest
3 cups/330g all purpose flour/plain
1 tsp salt
1 tsp baking soda
1 tsp cinnamon
1 can crushed pineapple, drained well
110g flaked coconut
110g chopped maraschino cherries
110g chopped macadamia nuts

1. Preheat oven to 350F/180C/Gas Mark 4.
Grease and flour well two 7 x
4-inch loaf pans. Beat eggs slightly. Stir in oil
and sugar before adding extracts, pineapple
juice and orange zest.

2. In a separate bowl, sift together flour, salt,
baking soda and cinnamon. Add to egg mixture
and mix just until ingredients are moistened.

3. Gently stir in crushed pineapple, coconut,
maraschino cherries and nuts. Do not stir too
much or bread will be heavy. Pour into
prepared loaf pans.

4. Bake for 45 to 50 minutes or until a
wooden pick inserted comes out clean. Let
cool in pan for 10 minutes before removing.

Walnut Fudge Bread

1 cup/225g coarsely chopped walnuts
12 cubes of chocolate
1 cup/225g butter
1 cup/225g granulated sugar
5 eggs
2¼ cups/225g all purpose flour/plain
1 tsp baking soda
1 tsp salt
1 cup/220ml buttermilk
1 tsp vanilla extract

1. Heat oven to 350F/180C/Gas Mark 4. Grease two 9 x 5-inch loaf pans and set to one side.

2. Toast walnuts on a baking sheet for 3 to 5 minutes or until fragrant, and allow to cool. Melt chocolate by microwaving on medium for 25-second intervals, stirring in between, until smooth. Allow to cool for 5 minutes.

3. Cream the butter and sugar, and then beat the eggs one at a time. Mix in with the cooled chocolate.

4. In a separate bowl, mix flour, baking soda and salt. Stir buttermilk and vanilla extract together. Add flour and buttermilk alternately to chocolate mixture, whilst stirring in walnuts.

5. Divide batter between the two prepared pans. Bake for 55 to 60 minutes. Cool bread in pans for 10 minutes, then remove from pans and cool on a wire rack.

Serve warm with fudge ice cream.

Kahlua Gingerbread

1 cup/200g butter
½ cup/95g granulated sugar
½ cup/110g brown sugar
1 large egg
1 cup/325g molasses
2 cups/200g all purpose flour/plain
1½ tsp baking soda
1 tsp ground cinnamon
1½ tsp ground ginger
1 tsp ground cloves
½ tsp salt
2/3 cup/160ml hot water
1/3 cup/75ml Kahlua
2 tbsp cold brewed coffee

1. Heat oven to 325F/160C/Gas Mark 2. Grease a 9 x 13-inch baking pan and set aside.

2. Cream butter and sugars together. Thoroughly mix in egg, molasses, flour, baking soda, cinnamon, ginger, cloves, salt, water, Kahlua, and coffee. Pour the batter into prepared pan.

3. Bake for 30 to 35 minutes, and allow to cool for 15 minutes before removing from oven. Leave on wire rack to cool completely. Serve warm or cold with whipped cream.

Marmalade Bread

1 loaf French bread
½ cup soft butter
½ cup orange marmalade
Cinnamon

1. Cut bread in diagonal slices. Spread with butter, then with marmalade (do not skimp). Sprinkle with cinnamon. Heat in oven at 400F/200C/Gas Mark 6 for about 8 minutes.

Sweet

Vanilla Bean Loaves

3 sticks unsalted butter, at room temperature
2½ cups/255g vanilla sugar (1 split vanilla bean stirred into 400g sugar; let sit for a few days)
1 vanilla bean
1 tbsp pure vanilla extract
8 large eggs, room temperature
3 cups/300g all purpose flour/plain
1½ tsp baking powder
½ tsp salt
Vanilla Syrup

1. Heavily spray two similarly sized loaf pans with non-stick cooking spray, and preheat oven to 325F/160C/Gas Mark 2. Cream the butter and vanilla sugar until mixture is pale and fluffy in a large bowl.

2. Scrape the vanilla bean and flick its seeds into the bowl, along with the vanilla extract and eggs; beat to mix. Sift flour, baking powder and salt into another bowl. Add to the batter and mix just until smooth.

3. Take a spatula to scrape the bottom and fold the mixture a few times, to make sure everything is blended. Divide the batter between the two prepared pans.

4. Bake for 30 minutes, then turn the pans around, and bake an additional 25 to 30 minutes. While the loaves bake, prepare the syrup in the microwave.

5. When loaves are done, cool for 10 minutes on wire racks, then turn them out of their pans and set back on the racks. Place the racks over a baking sheet and brush all over with the Vanilla Syrup.

Serve warm, with a scoop of vanilla ice-cream.

Sweet

Honeydew Bread

3 eggs, beaten
1 cup/225ml vegetable oil
2 cups/375g granulated sugar
3 tsp pure vanilla extract
1 small honeydew melon cut into 2-inch chunks and pureed (about 2 cups of puree)
3 cups/300g all purpose flour/plain
1 tsp salt
1 tsp baking soda
3/4 tsp baking powder
2 tsp ground cinnamon
½ tsp ground ginger
1 cup/125g chopped walnuts

1. Mix the eggs, oil, sugar and vanilla extract in a medium-sized bowl. Add pureed honeydew to mixture and mix thoroughly.

2. Sift dry ingredients together and add to liquid mixture. Pour into 2 greased and floured 9 x 5-inch loaf pans.

3. Bake at 325F/160C/Gas Mark 2 for 1 hour or until done. Check after 50 minutes.

Serve warm with whipped cream.

Sweet

Bourbon Pecan Bread

3/4 cup/115g raisins
1/3 cup/160ml bourbon
6 eggs, separated
1 1/2 cups granulated sugar, divided
2 cup/200g all purpose flour/plain
1 1/2 tsp vanilla extract
1 cup/100g pecans

1. Soak raisins in bourbon for 2 hours and drain, reserving bourbon. Add more bourbon to make 1/3 cup.Grease two bread loaf pans and line pan bottoms with greased wax paper. Heat oven to 350F/180C/Gas Mark 4.

2. Cream the butter and 1/2-cup sugar until light and fluffy. Add egg yolks, one at a time, beating well. Add flour in thirds, alternating with bourbon. Mix until blended. Stir in raisins, pecans and vanilla extract.

3. With clean beaters, beat egg whites until soft peaks form. Gradually beat in remaining 1 cup sugar; beat until stiff. Fold egg whites into batter, turn in to pans and bake for 1 hour.

Gumdrop Bread

2 cups/220g sifted flour
2 tsp baking powder
1/4 cup/75g granulated sugar
1 tsp salt
2 tsp vegetable oil
1 egg, slightly beaten
1 cup/200ml milk
1/2 cup/75g raisins
1/4 cup/45g Hazelnuts
1/2 cup diced gumdrops

1. Sift together flour, baking powder, sugar and salt. Add vegetable oil and mix the beaten egg and milk and mix with dry ingredients. Mix smooth without beating.

Sweet

Gumdrop Bread/Cont.

2. Dredge raisins, hazelnuts and gumdrops. Add to first mixture. Pour into well-greased loaf pan. Let rise 20 minutes. Bake at 350F/180C/Gas Mark 4 for 45 minutes.

Amaretto Coconut Bread
4 ounces tofu
1 cup granulated sugar
1/4 cup Amaretto
14 fluid ounces coconut milk
2 1/2 cups flour
1/2 teaspoon salt
1 tablespoon baking powder
1 cup unsweetened coconut flakes

1. Heat oven to 350F/180C/Gas Mark 4. Grease a 9x5x3-inch loaf pan. Blend together tofu and sugar thoroughly in an electric mixer or by mashing them together in a large mixing bowl.

2. Mix Amaretto and coconut milk into tofu until well blended. Meanwhile, sift together flour, salt and baking powder.

3. Throw in coconut flakes, then add the dry ingredients to liquid mixture and mix thoroughly.

4. Spoon batter into prepared loaf pan. Bake until done, about 45 minutes. Cool slightly before removing from pan.

Cinnamon Sticks

1 pastry sheet
1/3 cup margarine or butter, melted
3/4 cup confectioners' sugar
1 1/2 teaspoons ground cinnamon
1 cup chopped pecans

1. Preheat oven to 400F/200C/Gas Mark 6. On a lightly floured surface with a rolling pin, roll a pastry sheet into a 12x10-inch sheet. Brush with the margarine.

2. Sift the sugar and cinnamon evenly across the dough. Sprinkle with the pecans. Cut the 10-inch side into 5, 2-inch-wide strips. Roll up each of the five strips into 12-inch long "pencil" shapes.

3. Cut each of the "pencils" into 3 pieces. Bake on a lightly greased cookie sheet for 10 to 15 minutes or until golden.

Jam and Cheese Loaf

1 package dry yeast
1/2 cup/110ml warm water (100F/35C)
2 1/2 cups biscuit baking mix
1 tbsp granulated sugar
1 egg, beaten
1 cup/220g cream cheese
1/3 cup/75g granulated sugar
1 tbsp lemon juice
1/4 cup/60g strawberry preserves

1. Dissolve yeast in warm water, and let stand for 5 minutes. Add biscuit mix, sugar and egg, and stir well. Turn dough out onto a floured surface, and knead until smooth and elastic. Place in a well-greased bowl, turning to grease top; cover and chill 8 hours.

2. Punch dough down, and turn out onto a lightly greased baking sheet; roll into a 14 x 9-inch rectangle. Combine cream cheese, 1/3-cup sugar and lemon juice; beating at a medium speed with an electric mixer until smooth.

Jam and Cheese Loaf/Cont.

3. Spread mixture 2 inches wide lengthwise down centre of dough. Make 3-inch cuts into dough at 1-inch intervals on long sides.

4. Fold and over-lap strips diagonally over filling in a braided fashion. Cover and let rise in a warm place, free from drafts, for 45 minutes or until doubled in size.

5. Bake in an oven preheated to 350F/180C/Gas Mark 4 for 20 minutes. Remove from oven, spoon preserves down centre. Return to oven for an additional 5 minutes. Remove from oven and let stand for 10 minutes before serving.

Applesauce Cocoa Bread

Bread:
1 cup/100g all purpose flour/plain
3/4 cup/175g granulated sugar
1/3 cup/65g unsweetened cocoa powder
1 tsp baking powder
1 tsp baking soda
1 tsp salt
1/4 tsp ground cinnamon
Dash of ground nutmeg
1/2 cup shortening
2 eggs
1 cup/100ml applesauce
1/2 cup chopped pecans

Vanilla Glaze:
1/2 cup confectioners' sugar
3 tsp milk

1. Heat oven to 350F/180C/Gas Mark 4. Grease bottom only of 9 x 5-inch loaf pan. In a large bowl, stir together flour, sugar, cocoa, baking powder, baking soda, salt, cinnamon, and nutmeg.

2. Add shortening, eggs and applesauce, and beat just until blended. Stir in pecans. Spoon mixture into prepared pan. Bake for 50 to 55 minutes. Cool for 15 minutes; remove from pan to wire rack. Cool completely.

3. In a small bowl, stir together confectioners' sugar and milk to create vanilla glaze. Drizzle over bread.

Herb/Savoury
Breads

Prune Bread

3 cups/500 ml milk, scalded
3 tbsp butter
1 tbsp sugar
1 tbsp salt
3 tsp dried yeast
1/4 cup/60ml lukewarm water
6 cups/750g sifted flour
375 ml cooked, chopped prunes

1. Combine milk, butter, sugar and salt in a bowl and cool until lukewarm. Soften yeast in water and add to milk mixture. Add half the flour to milk mixture and beat well until smooth.

2. Stir in prunes. Add remaining flour to make a stiff dough. Turn dough on to a floured surface and knead thoroughly, for about 10 minutes, until dough is smooth and elastic.

3. Place dough in two greased loaf pans, and set in warm place to rise for about two hours. Bake at 350F/180C/Gas Mark 4 for 45 minute or until golden brown.

Black Pepper Crackling Bread

2 packets active dry yeast
3 cups/600g salt pork
1/2 cup/110ml warm water
4 tsp sugar
1 cup/220ml scalded milk
1/3 cup/75g shortening
2 tsp salt
1 large egg
About 6 cups/600g all purpose flour/plain
2 tsp ground black pepper
4 tbsp crackling
Melted butter for brushing

1. Cut salt pork into thin slices. Place in large baking pan and cook in a 450F/230C/Gas Mark 8 oven for 5 minutes.

Crackling Bread/Cont.

...eat to 350F/180C/Gas Mark 4 and cook for 25 minutes, or until ... and brown. Save fat for another use. Combine yeast, warm ... 1 tsp sugar. Let stand for 5 minutes to soften yeast. Combine hot ...hortening and cool to lukewarm. Add to yeast mixture.

... 3 tsp sugar, salt, egg and 2 cups of flour. Beat batter until it falls in a ...from the spoon. Gradually add remaining flour, kneading well. ...nue kneading on a lightly floured board until dough is smooth and ...y.

... Place dough in greased bowl, turning to bring greased side up to top. Cover with towel and let rise in warm place until double in size. Punch down dough and form into 2 equal sized balls.

5. Cover and let rest for 10 minutes. Roll each ball 1/2 inch thick in a 14 X 9 inch rectangle. Brush surface with melted butter and sprinkle with 1 tsp ground black pepper and 1 1/2 cups cracklings.

6. Roll up in swiss-roll fashion. Place in a greased loaf pan. Brush top with melted butter. Cover and let rise until doubled in size. Bake in preheated 375F/190C/Gas Mark 5 oven for 40 minutes, or until bread has browned.

White Sage Bread
2 1/2 cups/250g all purpose flour/plain
2 tsp finely chopped fresh sage leaves
1 tsp salt
1/2 tsp baking soda
1/4 cup/55ml lukewarm water
1 egg
1 cup cottage cheese
2 tbsp unsalted butter, melted
Crushed roasted pine nuts

1. Combine flour, sage, salt and baking soda. Dissolve yeast in the lukewarm water. In a food processor, blend egg and cottage cheese until smooth. Add 1 tablespoon of the butter and the yeast water.

2. Mix again, then transfer to a large bowl. Gradually add flour mixture, kneading vigorously after each addition, until a stiff dough is formed. Cover with a dry cloth and let rest in a warm place until doubled in size.

3. Punch down the dough and knead it on a lightly floured surface for about 4 minutes. Divide the dough in half and shape each part into a ball. Place the dough balls on a baking sheet, cover with a dry cloth, and let rise 15 minutes more.

4. Preheat the oven to 350F/180C/Gas Mark 4. Bake the bread for 40 minutes, until well risen, golden, and hollow-sounding when tapped. Brush the top with remaining butter and sprinkle with crushed roasted pine nuts.

Golden Cornbread
4 cups/500g yellow cornmeal
4 cups/400g all purpose flour/plain
1/2 cup/110g granulated sugar
3 tbsp baking powder
1 tbsp salt
4 eggs
1 cup/150g butter

1. In a large bowl, combine cornmeal, flour, sugar, baking powder and salt. Mix well. In a separate bowl, combine milk, eggs and melted butter. Add this mixture to the dry ingredients and mix well. Pour batter into greased 12 x 18-inch baking pan.

3. Bake in preheated 400F/200C/Gas Mark 6 oven until light golden brown, for 30 to 35 minutes. Cut into 2-inch squares. Leave on a wire rack to cool.

Green Tomato Bread

3 cups/300g all purpose flour/plain
¼ tbsp baking powder
1 tsp baking soda
1 tsp salt
2 cups/450g granulated sugar
1 tbsp cinnamon
2 large eggs, lightly beaten
1 cup/200ml vegetable oil
1 tsp vanilla extract
2 medium-sized green tomatoes, finely chopped
1 cup/200g chopped pecans

1. Heat oven to 350F/180C/Gas Mark 4. Grease and flour two 8x4-inch loaf pans. Combine flour, baking powder, baking soda, sugar, salt and cinnamon in a large bowl, and make a well in centre of mixture.

2. Combine eggs, oil and vanilla extract and stir well. Add to dry ingredient mixture, stirring until moistened. Fold in tomato and pecans.

3. Spoon batter into prepared loaf pans. Bake for 1 hour. Cool in pans on a wire rack for 10 minutes. Remove from pans, and let cool completely on wire rack.

Garlic & Cheese Flatbread

1 tsp active dry yeast
1 cup/235ml of lukewarm water
3 cups/300g all purpose flour/plain
1 tsp salt
1 tbsp white sugar
3 tbsp olive oil
4 tsp softened butter
2 tsp garlic powder
grated parmesan cheese
shredded mozzarella cheese

1. In a small cup, sprinkle the yeast over lukewarm water. Let it stand for approximately 10 minutes to dissolve completely.

2. In a larger bowl, stir together the flour, salt and sugar. Pour in the yeast mixture, followed by the olive oil. Beat with a spoon until the dough is sturdy enough to pull away from sides of the bowl, and doesn't stick.

3. Cover with clingfilm, and put aside until dough has doubled in size. Remove from the bowl and knead for 2-3 minutes on a floured surface. Roll the dough out to the thickness of your baking sheet.

4. Place on a greased baking sheet and spread butter over the top. Sprinkle with garlic powder, Parmesan and Mozzarella.

5. Preheat the oven to 350F/180C/Gas Mark 4, and when ready, bake for 20 minutes.

Bake until bread is golden and cheese is bubbly.

Herb/Savoury

Beer Bread

¼ cup/60g of melted butter
3 cups/330g of self-rising flour
½ cup/125g of white sugar
330ml can of beer

1. Preheat oven to 350F/180C/Gas Mark 4 Place flour, sugar and beer into a bowl and mix well.

2. Pour mixture into a pan, and bake for 40-50 minutes. After this time, remove bread and spread butter over the bread.

3. Place bread back in oven for 2-3 minutes. Leave to cool for 5 minutes, then slice.

Malt Bread

2 tsp fresh yeast
1 cup/220ml water
4 cups/400g plain flour
1 tsp salt
1 tbsp malt extract
1 tbsp molasses
2 tsp margarine

1. Blend the yeast into the lukewarm water and leave to stand until bubbling for 15 minutes. Mix flour and salt together in a separate bowl.

2. Warm the malt, treacle and fat until just melted. Stir both sets of wet ingredients into the dry ingredients - they should form a soft, sticky dough (add more water if needed).

3. Knead on floured board for 5 minutes, or until firm and elastic, with a little bit of bounce. Divide into two, shape into oblongs, roll up like a Swiss roll and put into 2 loaf tins, already prepared.

4. Leave to rise until the dough fills the tins (this may take quite a while, anywhere up to 90 minutes). . Bake in the oven for 30 - 40 minutes at 400F/200C/Gas Mark 6.

Ale Bread

2 cups/200g of all purpose flour/plain
2 tsp of baking powder
1 tsp salt
1 250ml botle of ale
1 handful of chopped shallots
1 handful of grated cheese

1. Stir salt, baking powder and flour together in a large mixing bowl. Add the ale. Stir in the shallots and cheese after this, mixing well throughout.

2. Knead bread briefly, and add a little more flour if sticky. Shape into a round loaf and place in a greased pan/cookie sheet.

3. Preheat oven at 380F/190C/Gas Mark 5. Bake at this temperature for 30 minutes, or until loaf sounds hollow when tapped.

Walnut & Parsley Bread

1 cup/125g walnut pieces
1 cup/150g strong wholewheat flour
1 cup/150g plain flour, plus a little extra for dusting
1 tsp salt
1 tsp easy-blend dried yeast
1 level tsp brown sugar
1 tsp walnut oil
2 tsp parsley
2 tbsp sultanas

1. Mix the flours, salt and yeast together in a large bowl. Measure 7 fl oz (200 ml) hot water in a measuring jug and whisk in the sugar and the walnut oil.

2. Pour the liquid into the flour mixture. Mix to form a dough, but if it appears too dry, add one or two more tablespoons of water.

3. Put the dough onto a lightly floured work surface and knead for about 5 minutes. Press the dough out into a rough 12 inch (30 cm) square, and sprinkle the dried fruit and nuts over the surface.

Walnut & Parsley Bread/Cont.

4. Roll up the dough, swiss-roll style, then knead briefly again to distribute the fruit and nuts evenly. Pat it out into a square and transfer the dough to the baking sheet.

5. Cover the loaf with clingfilm then leave this in a warm place until the dough has almost doubled in size. Pre-heat the oven to 400F/200C/Gas Mark 6.

6. Remove the clingfilm from the risen loaf and transfer it to the centre of the oven to bake for 35 minutes. Cool on a wire rack for 10 minutes.

Bread Sticks
4 cups/400g all purpose flour/plain
3 tsp butter
1 tsp salt
2 tsp yeast creamed with 1 tsp sugar

1. Sieve flour and salt into a pre-warmed bowl. Make a well, add a little of the milk to the creamed yeast and pour in, and stir in a little of the flour.

2. Allow to rise for about 15-20 minutes. Add the remaining milk with the butter melted in it. Allow to rise again for approximately 10 minutes.

3. Cut the dough into small pieces, roll into sticks 6-8 inches long and no thicker than your little finger. Place on a baking-tin and allow to rise for 20 minutes.

4. Bake in a 350F/180C/Gas Mark 4 oven for 20-30 minutes.

Traditional Breads

White Loaf

6 cups/600g all purpose flour/plain
1 tbsp sugar
2 1/2 tsp salt
1 tbsp active dry yeast
2 cups/440ml very warm water, about 120F/50C
2 tbsp softened butter

1. In a large mixing bowl combine 2 cups flour, sugar, salt, and yeast. Beating at low speed, add the water and butter. Continue beating at high speed for 3 minutes. Add 1/2 cup flour and beat for an extra 4 minutes.

2. Stir in 3 cups flour, or enough to make a soft dough. Turn out onto a lightly floured surface. Knead for 8 to 10 minutes, or until dough is smooth and elastic, adding a little more flour if necessary.

3. Place dough in a large buttered bowl, turning to butter top. Cover with a clean towel and let rise for 1 hour in a warm place, free of drafts. Punch dough down and knead until smooth.

4. Cut dough in half, cover with the mixing bowl, and let stand for 15 minutes longer. Roll each half into a 12x9-inch rectangle. Starting with the narrow edge, roll up, turning ends under to make loaves to fit pans.

5. Place rolls seam side down in greased loaf pans. Cover pans with clean towel and let rise in a warm place until doubled in size.

6. Bake loaves at 400F/200C/Gas Mark 6 for 25 to 30 minutes. Remove from pans to racks and brush with butter for a soft, more flavourful crust, if desired.

Whole Grain Loaf

2 tsp active dry yeast

1/2 cup/120 ml warm water (115F/45C)

1/4 cup/60 ml honey

3 tbsp canola/rapeseed oil

2 tsp salt

1 egg

1 egg white

3 cups/300g all purpose flour/plain

1/4 cup/60 g whole wheat flour

3 tbsp rye flour

2 tsp quick-cooking oats

2 tbsp toasted wheat germ

30 ml cold water

9 g sesame seeds

1. In a mixing bowl, dissolve yeast in warm water. Add cottage cheese, honey, oil, salt, egg and 1 cup of the flour and beat until smooth.

2. Gradually beat in whole wheat and rye flours, oats, wheat germ and enough remaining flour to make a soft dough. Turn onto a floured surface and knead until smooth and elastic, for about 8-10 minutes.

3. Place in a greased bowl, turning once to grease top. Cover and let rise in a warm place until doubled in size.

4. Punch dough down and let rest for 10 minutes. Shape into a ball, then place on a greased baking sheet sprinkled with cornmeal. Cover and let rise until doubled, for about 30 minutes.

5. Beat egg white and cold water; brush over dough and sprinkle with sesame seeds. Bake at 350F/180C/Gas Mark 4 for 25-30 minutes or until golden brown. Remove from pan to cool on a wire rack.

Brown Loaf

250g/9oz strong white bread flour, plus extra for dusting
250g/9oz wholemeal flour
200ml/7fl oz warm water
1 tsp of salt
1 tsp dried yeast
1 free-range egg, beaten
50g/2oz porridge oats

1. Mix the white flour, wholemeal flour, warm water and salt until well combined, then bring the mixture together to form a dough.

2. Turn out the dough onto a clean, floured work surface and knead with floured hands for 15-20 minutes, or until smooth and elastic. Shape the dough into one large loaf.

3. Transfer the loaf to a baking tray, cover with clingfilm and set aside for two hours, until doubled in size.

4. Meanwhile, preheat the oven to 450F/230C/Gas Mark 8. Once the loaf has expanded, brush the top of it with the beaten egg and sprinkle with the porridge oats. Bake the loaf in the oven for 25-30 minutes, or until cooked through (the loaf is cooked when it's golden and sounds hollow when tapped).

White Dinner Rolls

2 cups/450ml warm water
2/3 cup non-fat dry milk powder
2 tbsp yeast
1/4 cup sugar
2 teaspoons salt
1/3 cup butter or margarine, melted
1 egg
5 cups flour

1. In a large mixing bowl, mix together warm water and dry milk until dissolved. Stir in the yeast, followed by the sugar, salt, butter, and egg. (In the order specified).

White Dinner Rolls/Cont.

2. Add 2 cups of the flour, mixing with an electric mixer on low speed until moistened. Increase mixing speed to medium and beat for 2 minutes until smooth.

3. Add 2 more cups of flour, mixing on low until moistened and then on medium for another 2 minutes. Gradually add remaining flour 1/2 cup at a time until a soft, but manageable dough forms. You may not need to add the full amount. A softer dough produces a lighter roll.

4. Cover dough and allow to rise until doubled, about 1 hour. Punch dough down and roll into a 8 x 18 inch rectangle. Brush melted butter over dough. With a pizza cutter, cut dough in half lengthwise to make two strips, about 4 inches wide. Cut horizontally to make about 16 pieces of dough.

5. Starting with short end, roll up one piece of dough swiss-roll style with butter on the outside. Place in a greased glass pan.

6. Repeat with remaining pieces of dough, making sure that all rolls face the same direction. Cover and let rolls rise until doubled in size.

7. Bake at 350F/180C/Gas Mark 4 for 20 minutes or until golden brown. Brush with additional butter if desired. Cool in pan on wire rack for 15 minutes.

Stuffed Garlic Bread

1 unsliced loaf French bread
6 tablespoons butter
1 whole head fresh garlic. peeled and finely chopped
7 teaspoons sesame seeds
1/4 cup parmesan cheese, grated
1 1/2 cups sour cream
2 cups cheddar cheese, cut into 1-inch cubes
2 teaspoons lemon pepper
2 teaspoons parsley
2 cups chopped artichoke hearts

1. Cut French loaf in half lengthwise. Tear out soft centre of bread in chunks, leaving crust intact. Put crust shells on a foil covered cookie sheet, crust sides down.

2. Melt butter in a large skillet, stir in garlic and sesame seeds. Cook for 1-2 minutes on medium heat. Stir in torn bread chunks, and cook until golden brown and butter has been absorbed. Remove from heat.

3. In a very large bowl combine sour cream, cheddar cheese, parmesan, parsley and lemon pepper. Stir in artichoke hearts and toasted bread. Mix well and spoon back into bread shells.

4. Lay them both crust side down on the foil covered sheet, and put a sheet of foil over the top, then bake at 350F/180C/Gas Mark 4 for 20 minutes.

5. Remove foil and bake for an additional 10 minutes uncovered.

Let rest for 5-8 minutes before cutting.

Blueberry Bread

2 tbsp water
1/3 cup cottage cheese
1 tbsp butter
1/2 cup fresh blueberries
1 tbsp sugar
1 tsp salt
2/3 cup cornmeal
1 cups bread flour
1 tsp active dry yeast

1. Mix the yeast in a small bowl in warm water. In a large bowl, place dry ingredients. Add the butter, at room temperature, and use a knife to cut the butter into the flour.

2. Beat the egg yolks in another bowl, then add this to the flour mixture. Add the yeast mixture and add the milk, at room temperature. Mix thoroughly. Beat the whites of eggs until foamy. Add to flour mixture and blend, add enough flour to create a smooth ball of dough, but not dry.

3. Place this onto a lightly floured surface and knead for five minutes. Place in a deep bowl, covered with a kitchen towel, and wait for it to rise to the top of the bowl.

4. Remove the dough, portion into 16 or 18 pieces, and form balls which are then placed into two loaf tins coated in non-stick cooking spray. Cover this again, and allow to rise before baking at 350F/180C/Gas Mark 4 for 25-30 minutes.

Rye Bread

650g rye flour
5g baker's yeast
2 tablespoons yoghurt
1 tablespoon sugar
500ml tepid water
150g wholemeal flour
50g honey
1 teaspoon salt
7g brewer's yeast
3 teaspoon cumin seeds
4 tablespoons olive oil

1. Mix 300g rye flour, baker's yeast, yoghurt, sugar and 300ml water together to create yeast mixture. Leave overnight in a warm place for a stronger taste.

2. Sieve the remaining 300g of rye flour and wholemeal flour into a large bowl, then make a well in the middle. Pour in yeast mixture, with honey, cumin, salt, brewer's yeast, the remaining 200ml water and olive oil.

3. Stir well, then knead for 10 minutes, until you have a firm, smooth dough. Cover and leave to rise for an hour and a half, when the dough should have doubled in size.

4. Knead for a couple of minutes to bring dough down again, then divide into two loaf shapes. Place on a baking sheet, score each one twice lengthways, then leave to rise for an hour.

5. Preheat oven to 425F/220C/Gas Mark 7 and put loaves in oven to bake for 40 minutes, turning heat down to 350F/180C/Gas Mark 4 after 15 minutes.

Wheatgerm Bread

40g/2¾ oz wholewheat grains
100g/3½ oz wheatgerm
400g/14 oz wholewheat flour
¾ tsp fine sea salt
340ml/12 fl oz water, at room temperature
60ml/2¼ fl oz orange juice, at room temperature
40g/2¼ oz honey
1¾ tsp fresh yeast, crumbled
Olive oil, for greasing

1. Preheat the oven to 350F/180C/Gas Mark 4. Put the wholewheat grains into a saucepan over a medium heat and cover with water. Bring to the boil and reduce the heat to allow to simmer for 30 minutes, Remove from the heat and add cold water to cool the grains to lukewarm, then drain.

2. Pour the wheatgerm onto a baking sheet and place into the oven to bake for 11 minutes. Remove from the oven and leave to cool.

3. Place the flour, salt and toasted wheatgerm into a large bowl and mix together. Mix the water, orange juice and honey in a separate bowl.

4. Add the yeast and wholewheat grains and stir into the mixture well and dissolve the yeast. Add the flour and wheatgerm mixture and, using your hands, mix together to evenly combine. Cover and leave to stand for five minutes.

5. Flour a small loaf tin. Knead for five minutes, and then place back in bowl and allow to rise for 20 minutes.

6. Place the dough onto a flat floured surface and shape into a rectangular mould. Place the dough into the loaf tin, cover and leave in a warm (not hot) place for about one and a half hours, until it has risen half an inch over the top of the tin.

7. Preheat the oven to 220C/425F/Gas Mark 7. Use a sharp knife to make diagonal slashes across the top of the loaf and place it into the oven to bake for a minimum of 45 minutes, Allow to cool on a wire rack.

Buttermilk Cornbread
115 g butter
135 g white sugar
2 eggs
235 ml buttermilk
2 g baking soda
140 g cornmeal
125 g all purpose flour/plain
3 g salt

1. Preheat oven to 350F/180C/Gas Mark 4. Grease an 8 inch square pan. with non-stick cooking spray. Melt butter in a large skillet.

2. Remove from heat and stir in sugar. Quickly add eggs and beat until well blended. Combine buttermilk with baking soda and stir into mixture in pan. Stir in cornmeal, flour, and salt until well blended and few lumps remain.

3. Pour batter into the prepared pan. Bake in the preheated oven for 30 to 40 minutes.

Oatmeal Bread
1 cup seedless raisins
2 cups sifted all purpose flour/plain
1 1/2 teaspoon salt
4 teaspoons baking powder
1/3 cup sugar
4 tablespoons shortening
2 cups rolled oats
1/2 cup molasses
1 2/3 cup milk

1. Wash & drain raisins, and let them soak for a few minutes. Sift the flour, salt, baking powder & sugar together in a large bowl. Cut in shortening until blended.

2. Mix raisins & oats together in a separate bowl and add to flour mixture. In a small mixing bowl, combine molasses & milk until blended. Add to flour mixture and stir until combined.

Oatmeal Bread/Cont.

3. Grease & flour a loaf pan and slowly pour the dough into the pan, spreading it evenly. Cover lightly with a folded kitchen towel and let stand 20 minutes before baking.

4. Preheat oven to 350F/180C/Gas Mark 4. When heated, bake for 1 hour. Remove from pan and let cool on a wire rack.

Chocolate Chip Bread
2 cups all purpose flour/plain
1/2 cup baking cocoa
1/2 teaspoon salt
1 teaspoon baking soda
1/2 cup chocolate chips
1 cup chopped dates
1 teaspoon baking soda
1 cup boiling water
3/4 cup butter, softened
1 cup granulated sugar
2 large eggs
1 teaspoon vanilla extract

1. Preheat oven to 350F/180C/Gas Mark 4. Grease a loaf pan with non-stick cooking spray and set aside. In a large bowl combine the flour, cocoa, salt, 1 teaspoon baking soda and chocolate chips.

2. In a small bowl combine the dates, 1 teaspoon baking soda, boiling water and set aside.

3. In a mixing bowl cream the butter and sugar. Add the eggs and vanilla and continue beating until light and fluffy. Stir in the date mixture. Add the flour mixture to egg/date mixture, stirring just to combine, but do not over mix. Spoon into the prepared loaf pan.

4. Bake for 1 hour. Allow to stand for 10 minutes before removing from pan. Cool completely before wrapping to store.

Parmesan Herb Bread

2 cups warm water (110F/45C)
2 tablespoons butter
1-1/2 tablespoons dried oregano
2 tablespoons white sugar
4-1/2 teaspoons active dry yeast
1/2 cup plus 1 tablespoon parmesan cheese, grated
4-1/2 cups all purpose flour/plain
2 teaspoons salt

1. In a bowl add lukewarm water, sprinkle yeast over water. Let stand for 5 minutes, then stir and dissolve yeast. In a larger bowl add sugar, salt, margarine, 1/2 cup parmesan cheese, oregano and 3 cups of the flour.

2. Beat at slow speed for 2 minutes. Beat in rest of flour and cover the bowl with a damp cloth. Let rise in a warm place 45 minutes, or until doubled in volume.

3. Preheat oven to 350F/180C/Gas Mark 4. Lightly grease a loaf pan with non-stick cooking spray and set aside.

4. Punch dough down for 1/2 a minute. Turn dough into the loaf pan and sprinkle with the remaining 1 tablespoon Parmesan cheese.

5. Bake for 55 minutes. Cool on a wire rack.

Walnut & Sultana Bread

400g/14oz strong wholemeal flour
110g/4oz strong white flour
30g/1oz fresh yeast
15g/½oz salt
255ml/9oz water
85g/3oz sultanas
85g/3oz walnuts
handful flaked almonds

1. Preheat the oven to 400F/200C/Gas Mark 6. Mix the flour, yeast, salt and water in a bowl with your hands until it becomes a soft, pliable dough.

Walnut & Sultana Bread/Cont.

2. Place the dough on to a lightly floured, flat surface and knead for five minutes. Put the dough back in the bowl and leave to rise for an hour. Bring the dough out and mix the sultanas and walnuts into it.

3. Shape the dough into a loaf, and roll the loaf in flaked almonds. With a sharp knife, cut a line down the centre of the loaf.

4. Bake for 30 minutes, or until golden brown. Cool on a wire rack, serve toasted or with stilton on the side.

Traditional

Bread Machine
Recipes

Raisin & Hazelnut Bread

1½ cups/350ml warm water (105F/40C)
2 tbsp hazelnut oil
2 tbsp honey
1 tsp salt
1 tbsp non-fat dry milk
½ tsp ground cardamom
½ tsp grated lemon zest
3 cups/300g all purpose flour/plain
1 cup/130g whole wheat flour
3 tsp instant active dry yeast
Handful of hazelnuts
Handful of raisins

1. Place all ingredients except the hazelnuts and raisins in bread pan of your bread machine. Select dough setting and press start. After approximately 15 minutes of the dough cycle, add hazelnuts and raisins and continue dough cycle.

2. When dough cycle has finished, remove dough from pan and turn out onto a lightly oiled surface. Form dough into an oval, cover with a cotton towel and let rest for 10 minutes.

3. After resting, turn dough bottom side up and press to flatten. Shape dough into a loaf and place in a loaf pan that's been coated with non-stick cooking spray. Cover and place in a warm spot to rise for approximately 30 minutes or until doubled.

4. Preheat oven to 350F/180C/Gas Mark 4. Bake for 35 to 40 minutes or until loaf sounds hollow when tapped. Remove from oven and cool on a bread rack for about 10 minutes. Remove from pan.

Champagne French Bread

¼ cup/115ml warm water (115F/45C)
1 glass of Champagne, warmed
1 tbsp olive oil
1½ tsp salt
1 tbsp sugar
3 cups/300g all purpose flour/plain
3 tsp instant yeast

1. Place all ingredients except cornmeal in bread pan of your bread machine. Select dough setting and press start.

2. When dough cycle has finished, remove dough from pan and turn out onto a lightly oiled surface. Form dough into an oval, cover with a cotton towel and let rest for 10 minutes.

3. After resting, turn dough bottom side up and press to flatten. Fold dough into an envelope by folding the top 1/3 of the way to the bottom. Then fold the bottom a 1/3 of the way over the top.

4. Press dough with the palm of your hand to make an indentation down the centre of the dough and fold the top completely to the bottom, sealing the seam with the palm of your hand. Place on a baking sheet dusted with cornmeal. Cover and place in a warm spot to rise, approximately 30 minutes or until dough has doubled.

5. Preheat oven to 350F/180C/Gas Mark 4. After rising, slash the bread with a very sharp knife making three 1/2-inch deep diagonal slashes. Brush or spray the top of the bread with cold water and bake for 30 to 35 minutes or until nicely browned.

Buttermilk Bread

1 cup/200ml buttermilk (4 tbsp buttermilk powder and 1 cup/230ml lukewarm water)
1 tbsp olive oil
3 tbsp honey
1½ tsp salt
¼ tsp baking soda
3 cups/300g all purpose flour/plain
3 tsp instant active dry yeast

1. Place all ingredients in the pan of the bread machine in the order suggested by the manufacturer. Select dough setting and press start.

2. When dough cycle has finished, remove dough from pan and turn out onto a lightly oiled surface. Form dough into an oval, cover with plastic wrap and let rest for 10 minutes.

3. After resting, turn dough bottom side up and press to flatten. Shape dough into a loaf and place in a loaf pan that's been coated with cooking spray. Cover with plastic wrap and place in a warm spot to rise until doubled in size.

4. Preheat oven to 350F/180C/Gas Mark 4. Bake for approximately 35 to 40 minutes or until loaf sounds hollow when tapped. Remove from oven and cool on a bread rack for about 10 minutes. Remove from pan.

Raisin Cinnamon Bread

1 cup/230ml warm milk (110F/45C)
3 tbsp butter (softened)
3 tbsp ground cinnamon
3 tbsp firmly-packed brown sugar
½ tsp salt
3 cups/300g all purpose flour/plain
3 tsp instant active dry yeast
1 cup/150g raisins

1. Place all ingredients except the raisins in bread pan of your bread machine. Select dough setting and press start.

Raisin Cinnamon Bread/Cont.

2. After approximately 15 minutes of the dough cycle, add raisins and continue dough cycle. When dough cycle has finished, remove dough from pan and turn out onto a lightly floured surface. Form dough into an oval, cover with plastic wrap and let rest for 10 minutes.

3. After resting, turn dough bottom side up and press to flatten. Shape dough into a loaf and place in a loaf pan that's been coated with cooking spray. Cover and place in a warm spot to rise until doubled.

4. Preheat oven to 350F/180C/Gas Mark 4. Bake for 35 to 45 minutes or until loaf sounds hollow when tapped. Remove from oven and cool on a bread rack for about 10 minutes. Remove from pan and cool completely on a wire rack.

Sheepherder Bread
1 cup/230ml lukewarm water
2 tbsp olive oil
1½ tbsp sugar
1 tsp salt
2 tsp instant dry yeast
¼ tsp baking soda
½ cup/45g light rye flour
3 cups/300g all purpose flour/plain
Handful of sesame seeds
Cornmeal, for dusting
Olive oil, for glazing

1. Place lukewarm water, olive oil, sugar, salt, baking soda, rye flour, and all purpose flour/plain in the bread pan of bread machine. Process according to manufacturer's instructions for a dough setting.

2. When the bread machine has completed the dough cycle, remove the dough from the pan to a lightly oiled surface. Knead the dough several times and form the dough into an oval, cover with clingfilm and let rest for 10 minutes. After resting, turn bottom side up and press to flatten. Form dough into a circle and place on a baking sheet dusted with cornmeal.

3. Press sesame seeds into the surface of the dough and brush with olive oil. Cover with clingfilm and place in a warm spot to rise 1 to 2 hours until almost double in size.

4. Preheat oven to 425F/210C/Gas Mark 7. After rising, bake for 10 minutes. Reduce heat to 350F/180C/Gas Mark 4 and bake for an additional 25 minutes or until loaf sounds hollow when tapped. Remove from oven and place the bread on a wire rack to cool.

Fennel Bread
1 cup/230ml warm water (110F/45C)
1 tbsp sugar
1 tsp coarse salt
1 tbsp fennel seeds
2 tbsp extra-virgin olive oil
1 tbsp Anisette (anise-flavoured liqueur)
3 ¼ cups/325g all purpose flour/plain
3 tsp instant active dry yeast
1 to 2 tbsp olive oil (for topping)
½ tsp sea salt (for topping)

1. Place all ingredients in the pan of the bread machine in the order suggested by the manufacturer. Select dough setting and press start.

2. When dough cycle has finished, remove dough from pan and turn out onto a lightly oiled surface. Form dough into an oval, cover and let rest for 10 minutes.

3. After resting, turn dough bottom side up and press to flatten. Fold dough into an envelope by folding the top 1/3 of the way to the bottom. Then fold the bottom a 1/3 of the way over the top.

4. Press the dough with the palm of your hand to make an indentation down the centre of the dough and fold the top completely to the bottom, sealing the seam with the palm of your hand.

5. Place on a baking pan dusted with cornmeal, cover with clingfilm and place in a warm spot to rise for approximately 20 minutes.

Fennel Bread/Cont.

6. Preheat oven to 350F/180C/Gas Mark 4. After dough has risen, slash the bread with a very sharp knife making three inch deep diagonal slashes. Bake for 30 to 35 minutes or until nicely browned. Remove from oven.

7. Place the remaining tablespoon of olive oil in a small bowl. Brush the top of the bread with the olive oil and then sprinkle the salt over the top of the bread. Let the bread cool before serving.

Sweet Potato Bread

1 cup/250g sweet potato (cooked and mashed)
1 large egg
1 cup/230ml water (room temp)
2½ tbsp melted butter
2½ tbsp brown sugar
1 tsp salt
3/4 tsp cinnamon
½ tsp allspice
3¼ cup/325g all purpose flour/plain
½ cup/65g whole wheat flour
2 tsp instant yeast

1. Place ingredients into breadmachine according to the recipe. Set bread machine for a 2 lb. loaf, then press sweet bread cycle and a medium crust.

White Loaf

1 tsp instant dry yeast yeast
4½ cups/500g strong white breadmaker flour
1 tsp salt
1 tbsp granulated sugar
2 tbsp butter
1½ cups/350ml water

1. Place all the ingredients in the bread pan as listed. Programme for a basic bread and set to a medium crust

Bagels

1 cup/230ml water
2 tsp cooking oil
3 cups/300g all purpose flour/plain
1 tbsp sugar
3/4 tsp salt
1 tsp active dry yeast
1 slightly beaten egg white
1 tbsp water
Poppy seeds or sesame seeds (optional)

1. Add first 6 ingredients to a 2-pound bread machine according to the manufacturer's directions. Select the dough cycle. When cycle is complete, remove dough from machine. Punch down, then cover and let rest for 10 minutes.

2. Divide dough into 9 portions. Working quickly, shape each into a smooth ball. Punch a hole in centre and pull gently to make a 2-inch hole. Place on a large greased baking sheet. Cover and let rise for 20 minutes (start timing after first bagel is shaped). Boil, 5 inches from heat, for 3 to 4 minutes, turning once.

3. Meanwhile, in a large saucepan, bring 6 cups water and 1 tablespoon sugar to boiling. Reduce the heat and add the bagels, 4 or 5 at a time, and simmer for 7 minutes, turning once. Drain well.

4. Place on a well-greased large baking sheet. Mix the egg white and the 1 tablespoon water; and brush over bagels. If desired, sprinkle with poppy or sesame seeds. Bake in a 350F/180C/Gas Mark 4 oven for 35 to 40 minutes or until tops are golden. Remove from baking sheets and cool on racks.

Pitta Bread

1 cup plus 2 tbsp warm water
3 cups bread flour
1 tsp salt
1 tbsp vegetable oil
1 tsp sugar
1 ¼ tsp yeast

1. Place all ingredients in bread pan according to manufacturer's recommendation, and select the dough setting.

2. Turn the kneaded dough out onto a lightly floured surface and divide into 8 pieces.

3. Form each piece into a ball, tucking edges under. Cover and let dough rest for about 10 minutes. With a rolling pin roll each piece from the center to the edge, into a 6inch circle. Cover dough with a towel and let rise for 30 minutes.

4. Preheat oven to 450F/230C/Gas Mark 8. Place 2-3 pittas on a wire cake rack, and place directly on an oven rack. Bake for 4-5 minutes until puffed and golden.

5, Remove from oven and immediately place in a sealed paper bag or cover with a damp kitchen towel until soft.

6. Once softened, ptitas may be split and filled. Store in a plastic bag in the refrigerator.

Cocoa Almond Bread

1 cup warm milk
¼ cup butter, softened
1 egg
1/2 tsp almond extract
1/2 cup granulated sugar
1/4 cup baking cocoa
1/2 tsp salt
3 cups plus 2 tbsp bread flour
2 1/2 tsp active dry yeast

1, Put ingredients in in order listed by your bread machine's manufacturer. Choose your crust colour and loaf size if available.

2. Bake according to bread machine directions (check dough after 5 minutes of mixing; add 1 to 2 tablespoons of water or flour if needed)

Italian Herb Bread

9 ounces warm water
1 tsp salt
1 1/2 tbsp vegetable oil
3 1/2 cups white bread flour
¼ cup Parmesan cheese
1 tbsp dried parsley
2 tsp granulated sugar
2 tsp dried onion flakes
1/2 tsp dried basil
1/2 tsp garlic power
2 tsp active dry yeast

1. Measure all ingredients into your bread machine pan. Select the French bread setting and medium-colour crust, and press start.

Lemon Bread

2/3 cup old fashioned rolled oats
1 ¼ cups milk
1/2 cup lemon curd
1 1/2 tsp salt
1 1/2 tbsp butter, softened
3 cups bread flour
2 tsp active dry yeast

1. Place all ingredients in bread pan. Select Light Crust setting and press Start. If after 5-10 minutes it appears dry, add more liquid 1 tablespoon at a time until the dough is smooth and soft.

2. After the baking cycle ends, cool bread on wire rack for 1 hour before slicing.

White Chocolate Chip Bread

¼ cup warm water
1 cup warm milk
1 egg
¼ cup butter, softened
3 cups bread flour
2 tbsp brown sugar
2 tbsp granulated sugar
1 tsp salt
1 tsp ground cinnamon
1 (.25 ounce) package active dry yeast
1 cup white chocolate chips

1. Place all ingredients (except white chocolate chips) in the pan of the bread machine in the order recommended by the manufacturer.

2. Select cycle, and start machine. If your machine has a Fruit setting, add the white chocolate chips at the signal, or about 5 minutes before the kneading cycle has finished.

Jalapeno Cheese Bread

1 cup milk
2 tablespoons butter or margarine
2 diced jalapenos
2/3 cup grated jalapeno cheese
1/2 teaspoon salt
3 teaspoons granulated sugar
3 cups bread flour
2 1/2 teaspoons yeast

1, Add ingredients to the bread machine according to manufacturer's directions, using the white bread cycle.

Rum Raisin Bread

2 tbsp rum
1/2 cup raisins
1/2 cup water
2 cups bread flour
1 tbsp dry milk powder
2 tsp brown sugar
1 tsp salt
2 tsp butter
2 tbsp heavy whipping cream
1/2 tsp rum flavored extract
1 egg
1 tsp olive oil
1 1/2 tsp active dry yeast

1. In a small bowl, pour rum over raisins. Let stand for 45 minutes and drain.

2. Place ingredients in pan in the order recommended by the manufacturer. Use the regular setting for a 1 pound loaf.

3. If your machine has a Fruit setting, add the raisins at the signal, or about 5 minutes before the kneading cycle has finished.

Coconut Bread

1 ¼ cups fresh coconut milk

1/2 cup firmly packed brown sugar

2 tsp sea salt

1 tsp vanilla extract

¼ cup buttermilk or instant skim milk powder

3 2/3 cups unbleached white bread flour

2 tsp bread machine yeast

1/2 cup toasted unsweetened shredded coconut

1. Place ingredients into baking pan in order given. Set breadmaker to sweet dough or raisin bread cycle, adding the coconut at the beeper or during the last 5 minutes of the first knead cycle.

Brioche Loaf

1 3/4 tsp active dry yeast

1 3/4 cups bread flour

3 tbsp sugar

3/4 tsp salt

2 whole eggs

1 egg yolk

1/4 cup water

2 tbsp water

8 tbsp butter, unsalted

1. Add all ingredients except the butter in the order suggested by manufacturer and process on the basic bread cycle. Cut the butter into tablespoon-size pieces. About 10 minutes before the end of your first kneading cycle, begin adding the butter, 1 tablespoon each minute.

2. Let the machine continue its process. At the end of the entire cycle, let the brioche cool in the opened machine for about 20 minutes. This will keep the sides firm while the center stays moist.

Oatmeal Bread

1 cup boiling water
2 1/2 tbsp margarine
1 1/2 tsp salt
3 tbsp honey
1 tbsp dark unsulphured molasses
1/2 cup oats
1 extra-large egg, lightly beaten
3 cups bread flour
2 tsp. yeast

1. Measure all ingredients into machine according to manufacturer's directions. Use the light bread setting and medium-colour crust.

Tiramisu Bread

1/2 cup mascarpone cheese
1 cup coffee - strong and at room temperature
2 3/4 cups bread flour
2 tbsp dry milk powder
2 tbsp sugar
1 $\frac{1}{4}$ tsp salt
1 $\frac{1}{4}$ tsp yeast
1/3 cup chocolate covered espresso beans

1. Place all ingredients (except the chocolate covered espresso beans) in your machine's fully assembled pan in the order specified by your machines manufacturer.

2. Select the basic/white cycle and press start. If your machine's basic/white cycle doesn't have an add-in beep, then use the cycle that does or turn on the add-in beep.

3. Add the chocolate covered espresso beans at the beep or during the last 10 minutes of the final kneading cycle

Chocloate-Indulgence Bread

310 ml water
2 tablespoons oil
1 1/2 teaspooons salt
3 tablespoons sugar
450 grams (3 cups) white bread flour
2 tablespoons milk powder
1 1/4 teaspoons dried yeast
Nutella spread
2 (30 grams) chocolate flakes, crumbled
2 (50 grams) packets of Rolos
3 tablespoons hazelnuts, chopped

1. Select the dough setting. At completion of dough cycle, remove dough from pan. Place dough onto a lightly floured surface and roll into a square.

2. Spread with Nutella. Cut the square into two, then cut each half into 3 even-sized portions (6 in total). Sprinkle each portion evenly with Flake chocolate and hazelnuts and top with 3 Rolos.

3. Roll each portion as for a Swiss Roll. Place portions side by side in a lightly greased loaf pan. Lightly cover with clingfilm and stand in warm place until dough doubles in size. Brush with a little milk. Bake at 350F/180C/ Gas Mark 4 for 30-35 minutes or until cooked and golden brown.

Lemon Poppy Seed Bread

2 tablespoons lemon juice
1 teaspoon vanilla
2 tablespoons vegetable oil
2 large eggs
2/3 cup applesauce
1 cup sugar
1/2 teaspoon salt
1 teaspoon baking soda
1 tablespoon grated lemon peel
$\frac{1}{4}$ cup poppy seeds
2 cups all purpose flour/plain

1. Place the ingredients in the pan in the order listed. Select quick setting and start you bread machine. Keep the lid open and use a rubber spatula around the edges to be sure that the dry ingredients get completely moistened during the mixing time.

2. When the cycle is complete, remove the pan from the machine but do not take the bread out of the pan for ten minutes. Remove the bread from the pan and allow it to completely cool before slicing.

Focaccia Bread

1 $\frac{1}{4}$ cups water
1 tsp granulated sugar
3 3/4 cups bread flour
2 $\frac{1}{4}$ tsp bread machine yeast

1. Add ingredients to the baking pan according to the manufacturer's instructions. Select the dough cycle and start. Remove the dough to a lightly floured surface and cover it with a large bowl. Let it rest for 10 minutes.

2. Divide the dough into two equal pieces. Form each piece into a 10 by 8 inch rectangle. Flour your hands and use your finger-tips to dimple the dough. Cover the dough and let it rise in a warm, draft-free place for about 30 minutes. You can now cover the dough in any desired toppings.

5. Bake the dough on the bottom rack of a pre-heated oven at 350F/180C/Gas Mark 4. Allow to cool for 15 minutes

Garlic Parsley Bread

1 1/2 tsp active dry yeast
3 cups bread flour
3 tbsp wheat germ
3 tbsp wheat bran
1 3/4 tsp salt
1 1/2 tbsp sugar
1 1/2 tbsp vegetable oil
2 cloves garlic, crushed and minced
2 tbsp fresh chopped parsley
1 $\frac{1}{4}$ cups water

1. Add all ingredients in the order suggested by your bread machine manual and process on the basic bread cycle according to the bread machine manufacturer's directions.

2. Let the loaf cool before slicing. Serve plain or toasted with salad.

Tomato & Basil Bread

2 $\frac{1}{4}$ tsp active dry yeast
3 cups bread flour
3 tbsp wheat bran
1/3 cup cracked wheat
3 tbsp dry milk powder
1 tbsp dried leaf basil
$\frac{1}{4}$ cup chopped sun-dried tomatoes
1 tsp salt
1 $\frac{1}{4}$ cups water

1. Pour boiling water over sun-dried tomato halves. Soak for 10 minutes and drain, then cool to room tenperature. With scissors, snip into 1/4-inch pieces. (Do not use tomatoes that are packed in oil for this recipe.)

2. Add all the ingredients in the order suggested by your bread machine brochure and process on the basic bread cycle according to the manufacturers directions.

Hamburger/Hot Dog Buns

1 1/3 cups water
2 tbsp non-fat milk powder
4 cups all purpose flour/plain
2 tbsp shortening
2 1/2 to 3 tbsp sugar
2 tsp salt
1 packet yeast (about 2 1/2 teaspoons)

1. Add all ingredients to your bread machine in the order given (or according to bread machine's instructions) and set on "dough" cycle.

2. When cycle finishes, turn out onto a floured board and punch down. Knead 4 or 5 times; add a little more flour as you knead if necessary to keep it from sticking. Cover dough with a clean dishcloth and let rest for about 30 minutes.

3. Lightly grease a large baking sheet and sprinkle with cornmeal. Press dough into a circle and cut into 8 even wedges. Form each wedge into a ball then flatten into a smooth and fairly even circle.

4. Place each circle on the baking sheet and let rest for about 20 minutes. Bake at 375F/190C/Gas Mark 5 for about 20 minutes, or until nicely browned.

5. Shape these in a long narrow shape for hot dog or sausage buns, or make small shapes for party sandwiches. Serve with either Hot Dogs or Hamburgers!

Bread Machine

Almond Bread

1 cup milk
1 eggs
3 tbsp butter
8 oz almond paste
2 1/2 cup wholemeal flour
2 tbsp brown sugar
1/2 tsp salt
2 tsp yeast
1 tsp warm water
Handful of almonds

1. Pour the milk into the baking pan of your bread maker and break in the egg. If the butter is not soft, cut it into small chunks to ensure its blending into the dough, then add it to the liquids. Next add the almond paste, sliced so it will blend better too. Measure in the flour, brown sugar, and salt, and add the yeast as directed for your bread maker.

2. You can use your machine's full cycle with this bread, but the quick cycle is better. If a light colour setting is available, use it as well.

3. As soon as the bread has baked, remove it from the machine, closing the cover again, and ease the loaf from the pan.

4. Add the warm water and brush the top of the loaf with this mixture, using a pastry brush. Sprinkle the slivered almonds over the glaze, put the bread gently back in its pan, and return it to the bread machine for a few minutes to dry the glaze.

Cheese & Chive Bread

1/2 cup water
1 cup cottage cheese
1 large egg
2 tablespoons butter or margarine
1 1/2 teaspoons salt
3 3/4 cups white bread flour
3 tablespoons dried chives
2 1/2 tablespoons granulated sugar
2 ¼ teaspoons active dry yeast

1. Place ingredients in order given by manufacturer of your bread machine. Select Sweet or Basic setting and desired crust colour setting; press start.

Applesauce Bread

1/2 cup apple juice
2/3 cup applesauce
1/2 cup apple, grated
1 pinch nutmeg
1/2 teaspoon cinnamon
4 tablespoons sugar
1/2 teaspoon salt
1 1/2 tablespoons nonfat dry milk powder
3/4 cup whole wheat flour
2 ¼ cups bread flour
1 1/2 teaspoons bread machine yeast
1 tablespoon margarine

1. Add all ingredients to machine in order recommended by machine manufacturer. Select "white bread" setting and a medium crust colour.

Cherry & Raisin Loaf
200ml/7 fl oz of milk
3 tbsp butter
1 tbsp brown sugar
1 egg
1 tsp salt
1 tbsp ground cinnamon
400g/14 oz strong bread flour
1/2 tsp easybake yeast (for bread machines)
75g/3 oz dried cherries
75g/3 oz raisins

1. Place the milk, butter, brown sugar, egg, salt, cinnamon, yeast and bread flour into the pan of a bread machine in the order recommended by the manufacturer. Select the white bread cycle.

2. About 5 minutes before the end of the mixing process, add the dried fruit. If your bread machine has a fruit setting, use that.

Garlic Bread
225ml/8 fl oz warm water (45 C)
1 tbsp butter
1 tbsp dried milk powder
1 tbsp caster sugar
1 1/2 tsp salt
1 1/2 tbsp dried parsley
2 cloves garlic, minced and crushed into a paste
400g (14 oz) bread flour
2 tsp dried active baking yeast

1. Place ingredients in the pan of the bread machine in the order recommended by the manufacturer. select Basic Bread cycle and press Start.

Tomato Bread

1/3 cup water
1 1/3 cups tomatoes, blanched, skinned and chopped
2 tbsp olive oil
2 tbsp sugar
1 1/2 tsp salt
2 tsp parsley
2 tsp basil
1 tsp thyme
1 tsp oregano
3 cups flour
1 packet yeast

1. Add all ingredients to the bread maker pan in the order listed (or as directed in your bread maker instructions). Set bread maker to the regular setting and start.

Saffron Bread

1 cup milk
1/8 tsp ground saffron (1 package)
1 tbsp butter, softened
2 eggs
1/3 cup sugar
3 ¼ cups flour
1 tsp salt
1 package yeast
3/4 cup raisins

1. Add all the ingredients, except raisins, to the bread maker pan in the order listed (or as directed in your bread maker instructions).

2. Set bread maker to the regular setting and start. Add the raisins when the beeper sounds.

Rosemary Bread
235ml water
45 ml olive oil
6g white sugar
9g salt
pinch of Italian seasoning
pinch of ground black pepper
3g dried rosemary
340g bread flour
6g active dry yeast

1. Place ingredients in the pan of the bread machine in the order recommended by the manufacturer. Select white bread cycle and press Start.

Spiced Date Bread
1 ¼ cups water
2 tbsp butter
4 cups bread flour
¼ cup packed or
granulated brown sugar
2 tbsp wheat germ
1/2 tsp ground cinnamon
1 1/2 tsp salt
2 tsp yeast
1/2 cup finely chopped dates, soaked in hot water then drained

1. Add ingredients (except dates) according to your manufacturer's suggested order. Set on a light crust, then add drained dates at the beep.

Wholewheat Bread

1 cup water
1¼ tbsp butter
¼ cup brown sugar
1 tsp salt
3½ cups whole wheat flour
2¼ tsp quick active yeast

1. Add all ingredients to pan in order listed, except yeast. Form a small well in the flour, and pour the yeast inside.

2. Insert pan and choose whole wheat setting. choose desired crust colour and press start. When bread is finished, carefully remove and let cool.

Stuffed French Toast Bread

1 cup milk
1 tsp maple extract
2 tbsp butter, melted
3 cups bread flour
1 tsp salt
2 tsp active dry yeast
2 1/2 tbsp brown sugar
1/2 tsp cinnamon
1/2 cup dried apples, cut into small pieces
1/2 cup chopped pecans
1/2 cup cinnamon chips
2 tbsp nonfat dry milk powder
1/2 cup maple syrup

1. Place all ingredients in bread machine's fully assembled pan, and select basic or white cycle.

2. When fully baked, remove pan from bread machine and let cool for about 10 minutes before turning out and allowing loaf to fully cool.

Italian Dry Marsala Bread

2/3 cup dry marsala
1 cup golden raisins
1 cup milk
5 tablespoons butter
$\frac{1}{4}$ cup honey
1 teaspoon salt
1 1/3 cups cornmeal
2 2/3 cups bread flour
2 1/2 teaspoons yeast

1. Soak the raisins in the Marsala for at least 30 minutes. When the raisins have absorbed a good portion of the liquid, add whatever Marsala is left to the bread pan. Reserve the raisins for later.

2. Place the rest of the ingredients in the pan and bake according to manufacturer's instructions. Add raisins during the add in cycle or 5 minutes before the final kneading is finished.

Bourbon Nut Bread

$\frac{1}{4}$ cup vegetable oil
2 large eggs
1-1/2 tsp almond extract
1-1/2 cups sour cream
1/2 cup bourbon
1 cup packed light brown sugar
$2\frac{1}{4}$ cups all purpose flour/plain
2-1/2 tsp baking powder
1/2 tsp baking soda
1/2 tsp salt
1-1/2 tsp ground nutmeg
1 tsp instant espresso powder
$1\frac{1}{4}$ cups (6 ounces) coarsely chopped pecans

1. Place all the ingredients into your bread machine pan in order listed in manufacturer's instructions. Set crust for dark if your machine offers crust control for this setting and program for quick bread/cake cycle. Press start. The batter will be thick

2. After dough is mixed, scrape down sides of bread pan with spatula if needed to be sure all ingredients are incorporated.

3. Close lid and let baking process continue. When bread is finished, test to check its readiness. When done, immediately remove pan from machine, but let bread stand in pan for 10 minutes before turning it out, right side up.

Cool completely on a rack. Wrap tightly in clingfilm and chill overnight, or for up to 3 days, before serving.

Ricotta Bread

6 tbsp half-and-half
15 oz ricotta cheese
2 tbsp butter
2 eggs, beaten
$\frac{1}{4}$ cup sugar
1 tsp salt
3 cups bread flour
2 tsp yeast

1. Place half-and-half, ricotta cheese, butter, egg, sugar, salt, and bread flour into the bread machine except the yeast. Pour the yeast into the yeast compartment (or follow the specific directions for your bread machine). Bake the bread on the basic, non-rapid setting for best results.

(This bread is best served fresh and warm. Leftover bread may be used for homemade croutons or French toast.)

Multi-Grain Soybean Bread
2 cup bread flour
1 cup whole wheat flour
1/2 cup soybean flour
1 1/2 tsp nonfat powdered milk
1 1/2 tsp salt
1 1/2 tsp cornmeal
1/3 cup bran flakes
1 tsp flax seeds
1 tsp whole millet
1/2 cup soybeans, soaked overnight and dra
1 1/2 tsp soy oil
1 1/2 tsp honey
1 1/2 cup warm water
1 1/2 tsp dry yeast

1. Add ingredients to bread machine according to manufacturer's directions. Use a light bread setting.

Hot Cross Bread
1/3 cup water
2/3 cup milk
3 tablespoons butter, melted
2 eggs
¼ cup sugar
1 teaspoon salt
1 ¼ teaspoons cinnamon
1/2 teaspoon nutmeg
1/2 teaspoon allspice
3 cups flour
1 package yeast
3/4 cup mixed raisins

1. Add all ingredients, except raisins, to the bread maker pan in the order listed (or as directed in your bread maker instructions).

2. Set bread maker to the regular setting and start. Add fruit when the beeper sounds to add remaining ingredients.

"Special K" Bread

1 cup water
1 tablespoon liquid honey
2 tablespoons melted butter
1 teaspoon salt
1 1/2 tablespoons instant milk powder
2 1/2 cups flour
1 package yeast
1 $\frac{1}{4}$ cups Special K cereal

1. Add all ingredients, except the Special K, to the bread maker pan in the order listed (or as instructed in your bread maker instructions).

2. Set bread maker to the regular setting and start. Add cereal when the beeper sounds to add additional ingredients.

Tomato Herb Bread

1 packet dry yeast
1 tbsp sugar
1/2 cups warm water
1 1/2 cups tomatoes, peeled and chopped
2 tbs vegetable oil
1 tbsp fresh parsley
1 tbsp fresh dill
1 tbsp fresh oregano
2 tsp salt
4 cups flour
3 tbsp butter (melted)

1. Add all ingredients to bread pan. Set machine on dough cycle and press start. After the dough has mixed some, check to see if consistency is correct, add more flour or water if necessary.

2. When cycle is complete, remove dough from machine, form into loaves, and place into 2 greased 8-in.x 4-in. loaf pans. Cover and let rise until doubled, about 1 hour. Bake at 400F/200C/Gas Mark 6 for 15 minutes. Reduce heat to 350F/180C/Gas Mark 4 and bake for 25 minutes longer or until done. Brush with melted butter.

Pumpkin Bread

1/3 cup vegetable oil
3 large eggs
1 1/2 cups pumpkin puree
1 cup granulated sugar
1 1/2 teaspoons baking powder
1/2 teaspoon baking soda
1/4 teaspoon salt
3/4 teaspoon ground cinnamon
1/4 teaspoon ground nutmeg
1/4 teaspoon ground ginger
3 cups all purpose flour/plain
1/2 cup chopped walnuts or pecans, optional

1. Spray bread machine pan with a non-stick cooking spray. In a bowl, mix first 4 ingredients together until well blended.

2. Stir in the baking powder, soda, salt, spices, and flour just until mixed. Pour mixture into the prepared pan and set on the cake or quick bread cycle.

3. Add chopped nuts at the beep, if using. Carefully loosen the loaf and turn out onto a rack to cool.

Buckwheat Bread

¼ cup instant potato flakes
1/2 cup skim milk
1/2 cup water
2 cups bread flour
1 cup whole wheat flour
1/3 cup buckwheat flour
1 1/2 tsp. salt
1 1/2 Tbsp. applesauce
2 Tbsp. dark corn syrup
2 tsp. dry yeast

1. Place all ingredients in the bread pan. Select Light Crust setting, and press Start. After the baking cycle ends, remove bread from pan, place on cake rack, and allow to cool 1 hour before slicing.

Onion Dill Bread

3/4 cup cottage cheese
3/4 cup sour cream
1/4 cup water
1 1/2 tbsp butter
1 large egg
3 1/3 cups white bread flour
3 tbsp granulated sugar
3 tbsp dried onions, minced
2 tbsp dill seed, whole
1/4 tbsp baking soda
2 1/2 tsp active dry yeast

1. Place ingredients in the bread machine pan in the order suggested by the manufacturer.

2. Select Basic bread cycle and start machine.

Shredded Wheat Bread

1 1/4 tsp salt
2 shredded wheat; biscuits
1 1/2 tbsp wheat gluten
1 cup boiling water
3 tbsp boiling water
2 tbsp Wheat germ
3 tbsp Honey
2 tbsp Butter
2 cups all purpose flour/plain
2 tsp active dry yeast
3/4 cup whole wheat flour

1. Crumble shredded wheat biscuits into bread machine pan. Add honey and boiling water; stir and let stand 20 to 30 minutes, until lukewarm.

2. Add remaining ingredients in order recommended by bread machine manufacturer. Set controls for basic bread.

Index

index

Index

Index

Index

Index